web designer's guide to wordpress

PLAN • THEME • BUILD • LAUNCH

Jesse Friedman

Web Designer's Guide to WordPress: Plan, Theme, Build, Launch
Jesse Friedman

New Riders
1249 Eighth Street
Berkeley, CA 94710
510/524-2178

Find us on the Web at: www.newriders.com
To report errors, please send a note to errata@peachpit.com

New Riders is an imprint of Peachpit, a division of Pearson Education.

Copyright © 2013 by Jesse Friedman

Project Editor: Michael J. Nolan
Development Editor: Margaret S. Anderson/Stellarvisions
Technical Editor: Jonathan Desrosiers
Production Editor: David Van Ness
Copy Editor: Gretchen Dykstra
Proofreader: Patricia Pane
Indexer: Joy Dean Lee
Cover Designer: Charlene Charles-Will
Interior Designer/Compositor: WolfsonDesign

ISBN 13: 978-0-321-83281-8
ISBN 10:   0-321-83281-7

9 8 7 6 5 4 3 2

Printed and bound in the United States of America

For my loving wife, whose unparalleled tenacity motivated me to finish this book, and for my son, who teaches me more than I could ever teach him.

Download all the code and resources for this book at
http://wdgwp.com/downloads

Acknowledgments

I'd like to take this opportunity to thank not only those individuals who directly contributed to the making of this book, but also those who have motivated, taught, and inspired me over the years.

IN ORDER OF APPEARANCE

To my family, thank you for instilling in me the value of education and the importance of knowledge. Jake, you're an amazing friend, whom I know I can count on for anything.

Hilary Mason, thank you for the years of motivating, coaching, and teaching. You are a great mentor and friend.

Patrick McNeil, you gave me an opportunity to contribute to your amazing books, which both humbled me and open many doors. I appreciate our friendship and your continued support.

Jeff Golenski, I'm proud to have mentored you in the past and thank you for your massive contribution to this book. Your designs and photographs are amazing, as was your willingness to work with me at Starbucks into those late nights and even early mornings.

Michael Nolan, just months ago we were talking about this book over a box lunch and now it's a reality. Thank you for starting that conversation and for all your help with making this book a great resource. Margaret Anderson, I really appreciate your commitment to managing this process and all the late night and weekend hours dedicated to this project. To everyone else at New Riders who had a hand in this book, you're all amazing and I appreciate all your hard work.

Jon Desrosiers, you're a fantastic developer and, as it turns out, a great tech editor. Thanks for finding all the little nuances that I would have otherwise missed.

Sara Cannon, thank you for all your contributions to the WordPress community and for writing the foreword to this book.

To all the industry veterans, WordPress power users, friends, and colleagues who wrote letters for this book, thank you very much. To the rest of the WordPress community who literally made all this possible, I cannot begin to thank you enough. To everyone who has written a patch, contributed to the codex, developed a plugin, or run an event, you're an invaluable member of a global team. And finally, here's a special shout-out to @nacin, @markjaquith, @jjj, @janeforshort, @otto42 and, of course, @photomatt.

TO MY WIFE

Joy, this is as much your book as it is mine. Thank you for everything.

Foreword

In the past few years, I've been honored to speak at dozens of WordCamps, lead WordCamp Birmingham, and contribute to WordPress Core with the user interface group. I am honored that Jesse asked me to write this foreword. I love the WordPress community.

WE ARE PIONEERS

In this age of ever-changing technology, it's important to be forward-thinking. As web designers, developers, and builders, we need tools that are reliable, faster, better, and sustainable. We desire standards, yet also crave innovation. We don't want to sit idly while technology passes us by—we want to predict what lies ahead and make it.

WE SHAPE THE FUTURE

We need to protect ourselves and our content, and forge our own paths. We have to react to a constantly shifting landscape—proprietary systems only tie us down. To be forward-thinking, we need a platform we can mold into anything we want it to be.

WE USE WORDPRESS

We use WordPress because it's secure, reliable, and adaptable. It can fit anyone's needs, large or small—from high-traffic WordPress.com VIP clients to local urban farms. WordPress isn't just for personal blogs—it's the backbone of large businesses, tight-knit communities, web apps, and everything in between. Most importantly, WordPress is free and open source. Thanks to its license, the GPL, WordPress will remain free forever. The GPL lets you build on the shoulders of others, granting you the freedom to reuse whatever you want, shape it, and publish it at will.

WORDPRESS CAN DO ANYTHING

Not many platforms can do what WordPress does. Not many have the flexibility to scale and adapt. Some have proprietary code that you can't touch and remake into your own. With WordPress, you can remake and reuse—and you're not alone. WordPress is a community: there are millions of people just like you sharing their code, ideas, and innovations.

Jesse Friedman is one of these people. In this book, he takes you step-by-step through how to leverage WordPress and its intricacies, sharing the knowledge he's gathered from years of working with this tremendous platform. Jesse not only provides you with practical standards for WordPress design and development, but also dives deeper with his own insights.

Jesse has a knack for thinking about not only the outcome, but also ongoing usage. He shows great attention to how people interact with the WordPress dashboard, and provides insight into the user-admin experience. Pioneering the future requires more than a make-it-then-leave-it mentality—it takes thoughtfully crafting experiences for everyone, while keeping an eye on the future.

This book is a tremendous resource to our community.
—Sara Cannon

Sara Cannon is an artist, designer, and developer based in Birmingham, Alabama. She is the cofounder and creative director of Range—A Design and Development Shop.

Contents

The Letters

Dear WordPress Tenderfoot,

WordPress has evolved from a simple blogging tool to a feature-rich content management system, and even a web application platform. You can use WordPress to do almost anything, although it fits certain projects more than others. I've worked with many companies and individuals, architecting and implementing websites powered by WordPress since 2005. What follows are my recommendations for deciding whether WordPress is the right tool for the task and for approaching new WordPress projects.

When evaluating WordPress as a platform for a new project, start with the *information architecture* or the data layer. It's imperative to learn as much as possible about the information to be stored, how it will be organized, updated, and searched, and the relationships between data objects.

For simple websites, posts and pages are sufficient. However, more sophisticated websites often require custom post types. For example, an event will have a title, description, date, and number of tickets available. Post types may need to relate to one another—an event is associated with a venue, which has a name, address, and phone number. Custom post types often warrant custom taxonomies such as specific product categories. Custom post types, taxonomies, themes, and additional metadata can be added to WordPress fairly easily, but it's important to map out how they will be implemented and ensure that they meet the needs of the business.

Carefully review the website's *functional requirements*. An understanding of WordPress features will help you spot gaps where additional development or plugins are needed. When choosing plugins, it's important to consider: age (newer plugins may be less stable than competing, veteran plugins), compatibility (plugins should maintain current WordPress version compatibility), support (developer should be diligent in fixing bugs and responding to issues), and documentation (installation guide should be included, as well as usage information).

If, after evaluation, you find your project resisting "the WordPress way," you may wish to explore other solutions. This includes information architecture not conforming to the post type and taxonomy paradigm, custom theme and plugin development exceeding budget or timeline, or requiring more than 50 percent customization of the core.

As WordPress becomes more extensible, it will be a faster, easier, and more economical tool to solve increasingly complex client problems. May you find success and enjoyment in your WordPress projects.

James Coletti
jamescoletti.com | @jamescoletti

PART 1

WordPress, a CMS

In the next two chapters, we'll cover some WordPress basics. You may have used WordPress in the past; if so, that's great—we can build on that. If you haven't worked in WordPress before, that's all right because we'll start from the beginning and go over all the details.

We'll look at everything from why it makes sense to choose WordPress for your next project to how to install it on your server and add content. By the end of these two chapters, you'll have started an intimate relationship with WordPress that will last a long time. You'll get something out of these two chapters whether you're a veteran WordPress blogger or a novice who's never seen the WordPress admin.

When I started teaching web design, I had to cover every little detail of HTML, CSS, web standards, browsers, and more. I knew most of it already, but because I had to actually define growth paths for my students, I needed to know everything there was to know. This made me a better web designer, teacher, and business owner. I was able to explain the details of the web and my work with greater confidence because I could describe every aspect of what I was speaking about. You may know the difference between a WordPress post and a page, but in this part of the book, you'll learn how to explain it to your clients.

In Part 2, we'll build on our understanding of WordPress by diving into WordPress theming basics, template hierarchies, and best practices.

WordPress

Seven years ago, when I started with WordPress, I thought of it less as a tool and more as a requirement. My client needed a content management system (CMS) and I had grown tired of some of the other popular choices available at that time. Today I encourage my students and colleagues to learn WordPress, and you'll need to learn it if you want to work with me. That shift in thinking didn't take seven years; in fact, I fell hard for WordPress shortly after starting with it.

I hope that after you get through this entire book, you'll see what I see in this powerful CMS. If you're going to be a WordPress developer, or even a user, it's important to have a good foundation in its history, terminology, and usage. We're about to cover a lot of that in this chapter.

What you're about to learn

- The history of WordPress

- When to use WordPress

- A high-level overview of the design and development process

More than Blogging

Today there are hundreds of millions of websites delivering content to billions of visitors. We see social networks, content delivery sites like YouTube, blogs, business sites, personal sites, and even websites about your neighbor's cat Fluffy. Typical visitors don't realize the amount of work or the number of moving parts required for a website to run. As a web designer or developer, you have a better idea of what tools exist to help you power websites, and you're obviously aware that WordPress is one of them (you're reading this book!). You probably also know that WordPress isn't just a blogging CMS anymore. In fact, WordPress has emerged as one of the most powerful CMSs in the game.

> ■■■ **NOTE**
>
> In 2012, 22 percent of all new domains (websites) will be powered by WordPress.

Let's take a quick look at the history of WordPress so you have a context for the practical details you'll be learning in later chapters and are better equipped to talk the talk (**Figure 1.1**).

FIGURE 1.1 In the WordPress logo, WordPress is spelled with a capital W and P. This is the proper way to write WordPress.

History

If WordPress had a birthday, it would be May 25, 2003. Matt Mullenweg announced WordPress version 0.7 was available for download that day and, in my opinion, it should be a day remembered in history, or at least the history of the Internet. Later, Mullenweg formed Automattic, which is now the company behind WordPress.com and several free and premium WordPress plugins.

Currently, the WordPress Foundation manages WordPress and its projects. It's important to note that WordPress is distributed under the GNU General Public License. I encourage you to read more about the license here: **http://wdgwp.com/license.**

> ■■■ **NOTE**
>
> "The WordPress Foundation is a charitable organization founded by Matt Mullenweg to further the mission of the WordPress open source project: to democratize publishing through Open Source, GPL software." http://wordpressfoundation.org

WordPress.com and WordPress.org

If you're at a WordCamp or a WordPress Meetup and ask a generic question, a veteran developer might ask you to clarify whether you're referring to WordPress.com or WordPress.org. It's a simple way to understand whether you're referring to the free website hosting service, WordPress.com, or the software we download, develop, and launch ourselves, housed at WordPress.org.

Essentially, the software is the same. WordPress.com runs the same WordPress we know and love, it's just on a shared network. Remember the days of Angelfire and GeoCities, where you could sign up and build a free website? WordPress.com is like that. You can sign up, and launch your own WordPress-powered website for free. You can even point over your own domain and choose from premium themes. However, you can't write your own functions, build on functionality, or activate any old plugin. Since WordPress.com is on a shared network it limits what people can do, because one mistake could impair the entire network. As web designers we want more freedom, so this book will focus on WordPress.org.

WordPress.org has WordPress software available to download, as well as plugins and themes to activate and resources to educate yourself about the system. There are also forums, ways to stay on top of development, opportunities to contribute your own code to the core, and more. The software downloaded from WordPress.org requires you to have a server or hosting account and other essentials, which we'll cover shortly.

WordPress Resources

Chapter 20, "WordPress Community," goes into detail about the WordPress community, available resources, events, and ways to continue your WordPress education. In addition, reference websites and free resources are mentioned throughout this book. Below is a quick list of those sites and a little bit about them.

The **WordPress Codex** (**http://wdgwp.com/codex**) is a huge library of WordPress functions, calls, hooks, filters, and more. It's basically a WordPress manual written by the WordPress core development team and outside developers like us. There are educational documents, tutorials, and a "living repository" for general WordPress information.

WordPress Forums (**http://wdgwp.com/support**) are available to users and developers of all levels. It's wise to understand the different forums and when and how to publish to them. The forums are a great place to go when you can't find what you're looking for in the codex and you need help solving a problem.

WordPress Extend (**http://wdgwp.com/extend**) is where you go to build on inherent WordPress functionality. You can share ideas, report bugs, and learn more about how to publish from a mobile device. The biggest reason to visit the site is to download any of the approximately 20,000 plugins or 1,500 themes available for free.

Is WordPress the Right Choice for Your Project?

Well, I hope it is, because I don't want you returning this book! The truth is that WordPress is a powerful CMS that offers many tools, an easy-to-understand and robust application programming interface (API), and a large community of designers and developers contributing to make it better. WordPress has come a long way in the last few years, emerging as a full-blown CMS in late 2009 with version 2.9. However, to formally evaluate this question, we should make clear what WordPress is and what it's not.

What WordPress Is

WordPress is a CMS, which, by definition, helps you (or your client) manage and publish content with little knowledge of web markup or code. Whether you're a seasoned developer or a small business owner just looking to update his website, a CMS can help you by alleviating mundane tasks and barriers to publishing content.

WordPress is open source, meaning it's free and available to the public. While there are costs involved in hosting and supporting WordPress, the actual software is free and available to everyone. Open source also refers to the fact that the code, graphics, and other files that make up WordPress are readily accessible to anyone who wants to work on the CMS, improve it, or just mess around and learn from it.

WordPress is the most popular CMS used today. There are hundreds of CMSs on the market. Many are free and some are open source, but others are neither. WordPress has cornered the market, offering a free service to anyone who wants a website. Today there are approximately 72 million WordPress-powered websites on the Internet. No other CMS comes close to these numbers.

WordPress is fast, reliable, and scalable. If you're planning a website for hundreds of thousands of unique visitors a day, please don't simply dismiss WordPress. There are some really large websites with huge traffic numbers that are built for speed and growth. It may surprise you to learn that NBC Sports, CNN, *Time,* UPS, TechCrunch, CBS, and Mashable have websites powered by WordPress. Combined, these sites get millions of hits daily. Head over to http://wdgwp.com/vip and see other well-known sites and companies, if you're not convinced.

What WordPress Is Not

The following examples aren't intended to discourage you from using WordPress for these types of projects. Just know what you're getting into and understand what other solutions exist on the market before diving into using WordPress for these kinds of sites.

WordPress is not **an e-commerce platform.** Managing thousands or even hundreds of products is still difficult, not to mention tracking orders, conversion, inventory, and more. That said, many e-commerce websites are powered by WordPress. There are several viable plugins that build on WordPress functionality that can turn your site into a full-fledged e-commerce website.

If you have a WordPress website already built and you want to sell a couple dozen items, then plugins like WooCommerce (**http://wdgwp.com/woocommerce)** or WP e-Commerce (**http://wdgwp.com/wp-ecommerce**) can help you accomplish your goals.

WordPress is not **a web directory framework.** Managing huge directories in WordPress, like products in a store, is difficult. The user interface just isn't made for it. Of course, there are exceptions to the rule. In fact, one of my first WordPress out-of-the-box projects was building a 23,000-page directory that had to allow for searching, filtering, taxonomy, and more.

My Recommendation

With the advancements made in the API in the past few years, the number of plugins and themes, and the learning resources available, it's safe to say that WordPress should be on everyone's list. Is it the absolute right solution for you? That's hard to say, and frankly I'm biased. I have dedicated my career to WordPress, and because of the sheer amount of WordPress work available I have not had to build many sites using competing CMSs.

I could go on and on about the advantages of WordPress, but at the end of the day it's up to you to decide if it's right for your project. Knowing how to develop WordPress websites is an exceptional skill to master. With the number of WordPress-powered websites growing, there will be more and more WordPress projects and jobs out there.

Requirements

If you've come this far, you've probably decided that WordPress is the right tool for your project. Now it's time to discuss what WordPress actually needs to function. WordPress is built with PHP, a server-side programming language. PHP is also open source and there are countless websites, books, and resources dedicated to educating you on PHP programming.

> ■■■ **NOTE**
>
> I can hear the alarms going off in your head. You're thinking, "I don't know PHP and it seems really hard!" Don't worry! I've taught WordPress development to countless students who had nothing more than HTML and CSS experience. In most cases you can build a WordPress theme without even realizing that you're writing PHP.

WordPress Hosting Requirements

Here's a list of the hosting requirements: PHP version 5.2.4 or greater, and MySQL version 5.0 or greater.

Yes, that's it! WordPress basically needs a database and PHP to run. Most servers and hosting companies offer these basic services, often at very low cost. It's common to get a Linux server running Apache (the server software installed on most "boxes"), PHP, and MySQL for under $10 a month. You can read more about WordPress Hosting Requirements here: http://wdgwp.com/requirements.

Hosting Recommendations

I've worked with many hosting companies over the last 12 years and I keep coming back to one that's reliable and affordable, and that offers great support. Bluehost offers the hosting of "unlimited" sites for as little as $7 a month. Bluehost is great because it's super easy to use, offers automatic WordPress installation, and has 24/7 tech support that actually answers the phone. You can sign up for Bluehost at http://wdgwp.com/bluehost.

There are many more hosting companies out there and WordPress even makes formal recommendations, which you can read more about at http://wdgwp.com/hosting.

Site Planning and the Development Process

When you're developing a WordPress-powered website, the most important aspect to consider at the beginning is whether you're developing the site for one or many user admins.

> ### ■■■ NOTE
>
> I'll refer to user admins several times throughout this book. A typical static website will have a "user," that is, a visitor. However, anytime you're building a website that's powered by a CMS, you have to consider the user admin. This is the person who controls the CMS after the site has been developed. A user admin can be the web developer, the client, or someone who simply installed your theme. You can't know what a user admin will do with your product, but it's important to try and compensate for most of it, if possible.

If you're building a WordPress site for a single client, you'll likely have specific direction and details on exactly how the site should function. This means that you can plan and build your theme for exactly what is needed, eliminating a lot of extras and unknowns.

Developing a theme that you make available for public use greatly changes the scope of the project. You'll know far less and assume a great deal more. You have to make a conscious effort to plan for how a user admin might want to use your theme without bloating the functionality by attempting to compensate for everything.

Planning, Wireframing, and Designing

Since there are literally thousands of developers currently working on or with WordPress, there are many different processes to actually coding a theme. As with any website, I start with content planning and site architecture. With WordPress-powered sites, you want to spend extra time on this phase so you can correctly plan the use of content types, taxonomy, and more (all of which will be explained later in greater detail).

Once I have a good understanding of the site structure, I'll move to wireframing, then later to the design.

It's safe to assume that most small websites are developed from designs for a home page and single interior page. Since WordPress uses a series of template pages to display content to visitors, it's important to know what templates are available and how the content will be generated so you can properly plan for everything. For example, if you didn't realize that all WordPress websites allow for searching of content, would you design and plan for a search results page? Probably not.

At this point, I'll ask the designer to give me a set of design requirements for the browser. This way I can plan for all the available WordPress template pages without requiring extra work from the designer. If you don't design in the browser, then it'll be important to design your template pages in advance so your site isn't left broken or poorly planned.

Front-End Development

The next phase is development of the page templates in HTML, CSS, and JavaScript. I'll slice a design and develop the site in my browser. Before I move to actually developing a theme I'll code the site completely with static content. The goal here is to make everything work in all browsers set in your requirements and ensure progressive enhancement, site functionality, and everything else before we move to theming.

> **BEST PRACTICE**
>
> WordPress will frequently generate CSS classes on HTML elements. For example, when a user admin uploads a photo and inserts it into a post, he may choose to left-align it. The output <img> tag will have a class of alignleft. If you haven't declared the alignleft class, then this photo won't actually align to the left of its corresponding content. Luckily, the WordPress codex has a list of generated classes so you can properly prepare themes. Check it out at http://wdgwp.com/generated_classes.

I sometimes hear the argument that this process creates more work for the developer. I tend to disagree. When you gain enough WordPress development experience, planning for replacing static HTML with WordPress calls will become second nature. I know that I can plan for a site navigation using a <nav> -> <ul> -> <li> structure and simply replace that later with a WordPress call.

Once I replace the static HTML with dynamic WordPress calls, I'll have to do a little work to carry over HTML classes and IDs while ensuring that the HTML structure is the same. However, once I do, the HTML output will be identical to what I had before, which means the CSS will style the site exactly the same, essentially creating the exact same site.

I've been building WordPress–powered sites for many years and I've spent a lot of time on the process I'm about to walk you through. I'm open to new ideas, so if you see opportunities for improvement, I encourage you to get in touch with me.

What's Next

We just covered everything from the history of WordPress to hosting requirements to a high-level overview of the theme development process. In Chapter 2, "WordPress 101," you'll learn to install WordPress on your local machine and server, then get a down-and-dirty overview of the admin, adding content, and managing a site.

Dear Soon-to-Be WordPress Pro,

Hey there! So you've decided to jump into WordPress, huh? Welcome to the party. As a designer and front-end developer, I've had the opportunity to create countless custom WordPress themes and I've even designed custom themes for a WordPress theme company. My advice to you, as a novice WordPresser, can be described in one word: anticipate. Whether you're a web designer who can code or not, you're going to need to anticipate and design for possibility.

Possibility for what? What makes WordPress so great as a CMS is its ability to expand and evolve. The default installation is tremendous, but as you begin to work with it you'll quickly realize that your client's unique needs require some additions to WordPress. Of course, I'll leave all the fancy development shenanigans up to Jesse, but I want to talk to you about designing for expansion and additions with respect to widgets.

Widgets let you easily add content and features into designated areas of your WordPress site. If you've installed any of the default themes, you've seen a slew of widgets you can drag into the sidebar widget area. That's awesome! Sometimes. Because it's so easy to drag and drop elements within widget areas, it can also become a nightmare if your enthusiastic client decides to experiment and you haven't anticipated what he's going to change.

Imagine a call two weeks after your site launch. The client swapped out the search widget from the header and placed it in the secondary sidebar. He also removed the tag cloud from the sidebar and placed it in the footer. That looks terrible! The styles that you created for the element are not applied in this area of the site. Whoops. Now you have to backtrack and create styles for these widgets in the different widget areas. It's a bad scenario and it makes you looks bad.

The moral is, always take into consideration that the client can move elements around. When you design mock-ups, style common elements in each of the widget areas to give some design control over what will be placed there. And if the site is responsive, anticipate how these widgets will appear and function on different devices.

Cheers!

Jeff Golenski
golenski.com | @jeffgolenski

WordPress 101

WordPress currently powers over 70 million websites, with over half of them on a single network, WordPress.com. Among other great qualities, WordPress is fast, reliable, secure, and simple when it needs to be. On top of that there are thousands of designers and developers who are proud to be part of the WordPress community.

WordPress is quickly becoming the gold standard of content management systems. Its robust functionality is elegantly stored away until you call on it, which leaves you with an elegant, turnkey framework. Automattic, the company behind WordPress, has worked very hard to create a simple installation process that makes it easy for a novice developer to get started.

What you're about to learn

- How to install WordPress on a live server

- How to install WordPress on a local server

- WordPress security best practices

- The WordPress admin

- Expanding WordPress functionality, including plugins and themes

Installation

As we saw in the last chapter, WordPress offers two versions: WordPress.com and WordPress.org. With WordPress.com, you can build a free, hosted site or blog in minutes and be on your way. You can use your own domain and you don't need your own server, but your ability to expand is limited. You can choose only from preapproved plugins and themes and you can't write custom code.

WordPress.org offers a more robust site filled with information, directories of plugins and themes, and a codex outlining exactly how to build and improve on WordPress. From there you can download WordPress so you can install it on your own server.

It's important to know the difference and to become familiar with both versions; however, we'll be using only WordPress.org in this book.

Downloading WordPress

As we progress through the book we'll be working with specific files and examples, which will help you focus on learning WordPress. To get started head over to WordPress.org and click the rather conspicuous Download WordPress button. The next page tells you a little more about the WordPress installation process and gives you a choice between downloading a .zip or a .tar.gz file. Either is fine. Download the files, unpack them, and open the folder (**Figure 2.1**).

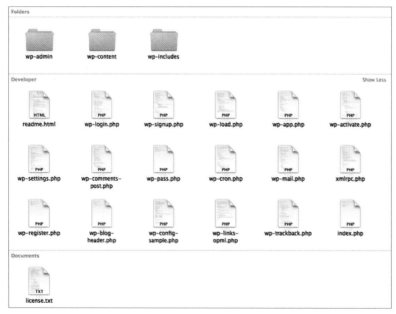

FIGURE 2.1 WordPress file structure.

When you open the folder structure, you'll see several administrative files and three folders. During the installation process you need be concerned with only one file: wp-config-sample.php, which we'll rename to wp-config.php for proper referencing.

Avoid editing the files in the wp-admin and wp-includes. The files in wp-admin and wp-includes are often referred to as the "core" and should not be altered. Doing so is referred to as "hacking the core," and we can avoid this by leveraging the API. The wp-content folder neatly houses all your additions, including theme files, plugins, any uploaded media, and so on.

■■■ NOTE

If you've never worked in WordPress before I suggest you a do a second WordPress installation just to mess around. I would add content, upload photos, and create widgets and anything else you can think of. I'd even start editing or modifying one of the default templates so you can get an idea of how things work. You can do this by going to Appearance → Editor.

This is essential because messing around with the settings and theme files may break the site or cause problems later. Have fun in WordPress without stress and then when you're ready to move into development, jump back over to the clean installation.

Installation Basics

Whether you're working on a local server or an actual web server, the installation process is the same. If you're not working from a local server I recommend you start today. There are some great free solutions for both PC and Mac users.

On a PC I prefer WAMP (http://wdgwp.com/wamp) and on a Mac I use MAMP (http://wdgwp.com/mamp). Either choice is fine and both will give you a web-server environment on your local machine, which basically means you don't have to FTP your files to the server to test your PHP code every time you make a change. This goes a long way to saving you time and aggravation.

> **BEST PRACTICE**
>
> When possible, work from a local environment when developing themes and plugins. Local server software gives you the experience of working on a live web server from the comfort of your computer. There are several benefits, including no need to FTP files, no need for an Internet connection, faster development times, and more.

The text below is taken from the instructions found on WordPress.org. You can find further detailed installation instructions and help at **http://wdgwp.com/install**. I'd also recommend researching database creation and security to learn more about good naming conventions and ways to create complex passwords to prevent theft.

FAMOUS 5-MINUTE INSTALL

Here's the quick version of the instructions, for those that are already comfortable with performing such installations.

If you are not comfortable with renaming files, Steps 3 and 4 are optional and you can skip them as the install program will create wp-config.php file.

1. Download and unzip the WordPress package if you haven't already.
2. Create a database for WordPress on your web server, as well as a MySQL user who has all privileges for accessing and modifying it.
3. Rename the wp-config-sample.php file to wp-config.php.
4. Open wp-config.php in a text editor and fill in your database details as explained in Editing wp-config.php to generate and use your secret key password.
5. Upload the WordPress files in the desired location on your web server:
   - If you want to integrate WordPress into the root of your domain (e.g., http://example.com/), move or upload all contents of the unzipped WordPress directory (but excluding the directory itself) into the root directory of your web server.
   - If you want to have your WordPress installation in its own subdirectory on your web site (e.g., http://example.com/blog/), create the blog directory on your server and upload WordPress to the directory via FTP.
6. Run the WordPress installation script by accessing wp-admin/install.php in a web browser.
   - If you installed WordPress in the root directory, you should visit: http://example.com/wp-admin/install.php
   - If you installed WordPress in its own subdirectory called blog, for example, you should visit:http://example.com/blog/wp-admin/install.php

That's it! WordPress should now be installed.

WordPress Installation on MAMP

If you're going to spend a lot of time designing and developing themes for WordPress, it's wise to be as efficient as possible. Utilizing a local server environment like MAMP will take the pain out of working on a server by letting you keep your files locally on your machine. MAMP simply means Mac, Apache, mysql and PHP (if you are on Windows there is WAMP).

To install WordPress, start by turning on MAMP and locating your file directory. Create a new folder to house your new website. Next, simply drag and drop all the files in the recent WordPress folder into this new directory. Once the file transfer is complete, navigate to your site via a web browser (typically http://localhost/folder-name), where you should be presented with an error (**Figure** 2.3). This error is actually the first step in the installation process. The lack of a wp-config.php file means that WordPress cannot connect to your database.

FIGURE 2.3
Missing wp-config.php error.

Clicking the Create a Configuration File button takes you to the preparation screen (**Figure** 2.4). Here you're notified of what you need to do to continue the installation process. You'll need to create a database in advance, and you can do that by going to http://localhost/MAMP/ and clicking phpMyAdmin at the top.

FIGURE 2.4
WordPress installation prep screen.

Since we're installing on MAMP, the database username and password are both "root." The database host is, of course, "localhost." We can choose a table prefix on the fly. By default, the table prefix is set to wp_, which you should change for security reasons. If everyone knows that by default the table prefix is wp_, then everyone knows that your options table is called wp_options. Changing the prefix of your tables gives you an additional layer of security. The next screen asks you to simply input that data and click Submit (**Figure 2.5**).

FIGURE 2.5
Database information.

On the next screen, click the Run the install button and WordPress automatically generates the wp-config.php file for you (**Figure 2.6**). Once this is done, WordPress can communicate to the database, create the necessary tables, and set up the admin.

FIGURE 2.6
WordPress "Run the install" button.

Immediately following the installation you're asked to name your site and set up the admin account to manage the site (**Figure 2.7**). By default the username is "admin" but again for security purposes it's important to be as unpredictable as possible, so choose a different username. If you've already installed WordPress, it's important to save the admin account but change its role. We'll discuss this in greater detail later in this chapter.

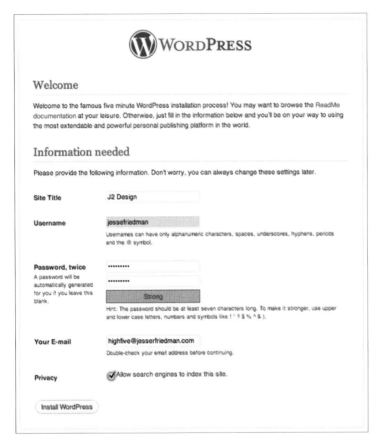

FIGURE 2.7
WordPress welcome
screen.

The next screen should show you a message of "Success!" and then give you an opportunity to log in (Figure 2.8). If you don't see a successful install message something has gone horribly wrong. I'm only joking—it probably means you had a slight error along the way and if you go back and double-check everything you should be good to go.

FIGURE 2.8
Installation success.

Remember, now that WordPress is installed locally, you can access the admin and login screen by going to http://localhost/directory/wp-admin (**Figure** 2.9).

FIGURE 2.9
WordPress login.

Additional Security Measures

In addition to the secret key (mentioned in Step 4 of the "Installation Basics" section), there are a few other elements you should modify in the wp-config.php file to increase security.

> **BEST PRACTICE**
>
> What follows are some important security measures to take. If you followed the installation process outlined above where WordPress generates the wp-config.php file on your behalf, you can probably skip this entire section. It is, however, important to read and follow along for your own experience.

On lines 45–52 of wp-config.php you'll see an opportunity to define Unique Keys and Salts. When done right, these phrases make it much more difficult for someone to hack into your WordPress install. You don't have to remember your phrases or even generate them. On line 40 you'll see a URL where WordPress generates the phrases for you. Simply go to **https://api.wordpress.org/secret-key/1.1/salt/** and copy and paste the generated phrases over the existing temporary code. See below:

Before:

```
define('AUTH_KEY',         'put your unique phrase here');
define('SECURE_AUTH_KEY',  'put your unique phrase here');
define('LOGGED_IN_KEY',    'put your unique phrase here');
define('NONCE_KEY',        'put your unique phrase here');
define('AUTH_SALT',        'put your unique phrase here');
define('SECURE_AUTH_SALT', 'put your unique phrase here');
define('LOGGED_IN_SALT',   'put your unique phrase here');
define('NONCE_SALT',       'put your unique phrase here');
```

After:

```
define('AUTH_KEY', 'Y9Nld_2V16aL<Cn)fXl_r>J?NsgL0.>>]yVwzLA?/*XgXyq|!Lr+)09;
        X@{Gr[{w');
define('SECURE_AUTH_KEY', 'nswG|=(CT6D0fe#LM0;(luHo58`E/-946h|TTr-VnoN}
        A/-3s^ISHYKGmQU6.q}');
define('LOGGED_IN_KEY', 'sh9TS9[>R<2@d0;Q83@*ll$2c<-_c._^*YN~:uS.Kz4>J.aYy;
        iT&gt3N| ezq>s');
define('NONCE_KEY', '?^&p!rx-FCN0Y OrGBTxc]2zJ-A6t|}~}{|$sG-khLm|7*/
        x<7~a;2&cGe|M4~1L');
define('AUTH_SALT', 'a#2U>SrcK0`dxh39z;3vp^LyyP_Z]dNQij+?zVWNmQ*NpgZa-,
        o5=(cAZ%tRa>X$');
define('SECURE_AUTH_SALT', 'r_ls~DpDE*g{}h9ywjG5H;wa_YP*<*FB9|UTAtbwR22+AQfP>
        gNY>bhUtXJe=)G');
define('LOGGED_IN_SALT', 'b:{.-j8|us6m(IViS,}*Sd|:DpoDEwhZo_m]
        ygwy+!N>`;Ku`dT#T`K;qAxNQ[6f');
define('NONCE_SALT', 'g-hvv(VeqXz#:r}M.?YZKd,NKfa,s[SlkwP^KoM++X#nU+]
        iWY,>K-<>,Tu!hwq|');
```

The next change is on line 62 of wp-config.php, which is for table prefix. You already created your database and assigned a user. Hopefully, you created a complex database name and an extremely difficult password. WordPress will create all the tables you need in your database. The names of these tables are always the same and start with the table prefix, which by default is "wp_", which means that in the unlikely event someone was able to access your database, she would know exactly what tables to modify to take down or damage your site.

It's good practice to change your table prefix to something complicated and unpredictable in an effort to further thwart hackers. As you can see below, I changed my table prefix to an abbreviated site name.

Before:

```
$table_prefix = 'wp_';
```

After:

```
$table_prefix = 'j2d_';
```

The final piece of code to change in wp-config.php is on line 81. We're changing the value of WP_DEBUG from "false" to "true." Setting debug to true alerts you of errors or warnings throughout the development process. When you're ready to go live, you'll set this back to false:

```
define('WP_DEBUG', false);
define('WP_DEBUG', true);
```

At this point you should be off and running. Your WordPress installation is complete, and you can now log in to your WordPress website.

Getting to Know WordPress

In an effort to create a unified foundation of WordPress knowledge, we'll now look at some of the more common areas of the WordPress admin. If you're well versed in WordPress, feel free to skip this section and just refer back later when you need specifics. We are going to walk through the admin area, how to create content, change settings, and more.

Toolbar

The Toolbar appears at the top of your screen at all times and is rather helpful, see (2) in Figure 2.10. Rolling over the WordPress logo on the left helps you find important documentation and help. You can also quickly view the front end of your websites, see if there are any site, theme, or plugin updates, and more. Take some time to investigate the toolbar because it will help you navigate your site much more quickly. My favorite use is the "+New" drop-down menu, which makes it very easy to start writing a new post.

■■■ NOTE

You can turn off the WordPress Toolbar when viewing the site by going to your user profile and setting it in the options. While the toolbar does offer some convenience, it can get in the way of your design when you're building.

Dashboard

The WordPress dashboard is exactly that, a dashboard, as shown in Figure 2.10. It gives you a quick rundown of the happenings of your WordPress website. The screenshot to the right shows you the default layout of the dashboard, most notably the Right Now section (1).

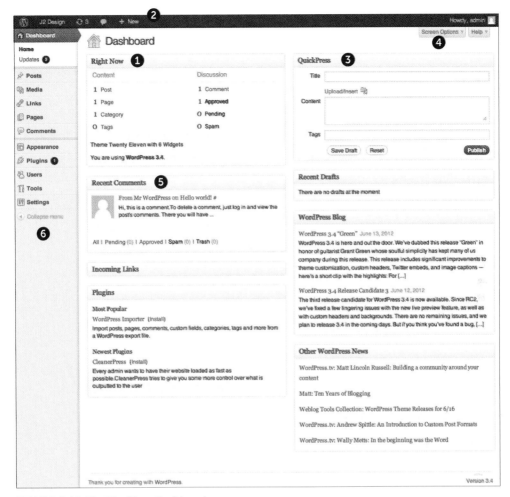

FIGURE 2.10 The WordPress Dashboard.

Right now there is one post, one page, and one category—you get the idea. It also tells you the theme that's currently activated, the number of widgets being used, and the current version of WordPress. This little window helps you keep your finger on the pulse of your website.

QuickPress (3) lets you quickly publish a post. I rarely use this to write posts, but it's an easy way to jot down ideas, save them, and return to them later. I'll often come up with an idea for a new post but don't have time to write the whole thing at that moment.

The other windows are pretty self-explanatory and include news and updates on WordPress and other information about your site. You can see a list of your most recent comments and their status under Recent Comments (5).

You can easily edit the dashboard with your own personal preferences. You can shrink windows, rearrange them, or remove them completely. You may also find new windows added to your dashboard in the future, because some plugins and themes modify the dashboard with additional options and data.

To modify your dashboard to your liking, start by clicking the Screen Options tab in the top right (4). From there you can turn on and off specific windows and even change the number of columns. I prefer a three-column layout as I work with a wider screen. To rearrange the dashboard windows simply drag and drop them until you find the order and layout you like.

The menu on the left houses the main navigation (6). You can collapse this menu if you prefer to have a slightly less cluttered dashboard.

Posts

Bloggers will spend the majority of their time in the Posts section (**Figure 2.11**). A post is a content entry that, unlike a page, usually lets users comment and has a time and date associated with it. Posts are typically displayed in reverse chronological order throughout the site. Posts can also belong to a category and be associated with tags.

FIGURE 2.11 Posts screen.

Categories and tags allow for organization and grouping of content. Users can sort and filter posts by categories and tags on sites that make this available. I prefer to use categories as broad generalizations like "article" or "tutorial," then get more specific with tags.

Adding content to a post is simple. **Figure 2.12** outlines the different sections of content. For a user admin, adding content is similar to working in Microsoft Word or other word processing software. You also have the option for HTML input if you have those skills. It's good practice to limit the use of HTML coding in posts as you don't want user admins to have to know HTML to add or edit content on their sites or blogs.

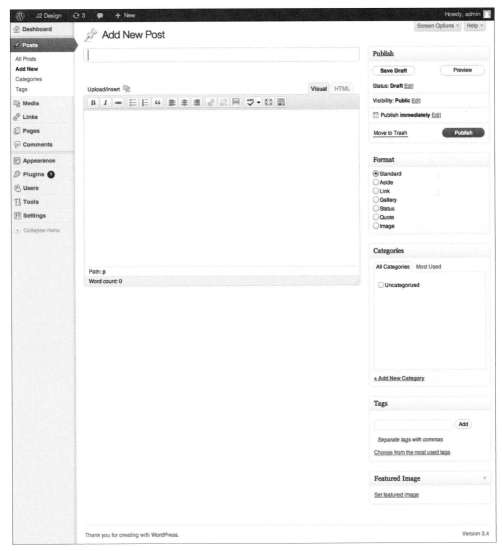

FIGURE 2.12 Adding a new post.

Media

Media can be added in the Media section of the WordPress admin or, more commonly, directly through the content editor. Typically you'll be adding images, videos, audio, and more directly to a post or page when you're creating or editing the content. However, the Media section works conveniently as a library where you can find images you've uploaded and gather more helpful data.

The Media section is an area of WordPress that leaves a lot to be desired. Until WordPress core developers build on this section to include helpful functions it's unlikely you'll be spending a great deal of time here.

Since we just installed WordPress you won't have any images loaded into the media library just yet. Soon you'll see thumbnails, PDFs, and other forms of media in the library after you've uploaded them to posts and pages.

Clicking on a thumbnail provides vital information, including available image sizes, the full-size image URL, and so forth.

When adding an image to the content editor, the user admin gains some additional functionality. She can choose to insert the image into the post, and decide how it will be aligned, its size, and whether it's linked to another page or itself. Once the image is added to the content editor the user admin can click on the image to resize it further or even change its alignment.

Links

The Links section of WordPress allows for easy addition of a list of outside links. A lawyer might use links to all her affiliations and licenses. A mommy blogger might link to fellow bloggers or even paid partners. You can utilize links for any practical purpose and there are several additional meta fields so you can associate links and more.

I personally don't use the Links section because I find it far easier to create a custom menu. A user admin will likely find it easier to create a menu than a link list as well.

We'll look at how to create menus later in this chapter. If you have many links to add to your site, it might be easier to use the Inherit Link feature rather than creating a custom menu. In any case, you should understand the Links section so that option is available to you.

Pages

Browse to the Edit Page page. As you can see, the term "page" can be confusing at times. We refer to pages as single displayed pages on the screen. The home page, Archives page, Post page, and Search Results page are web pages, but they are also template pages. The terminology can become redundant and confusing. The difference between a page of content and a post is typically defined as a page being static or permanent.

Pages share much of the same functionality as a post. Both have a title, slug (uri), content editor, date, and more. A page, however, does not reside in a category and usually can't be tagged. Instead, pages have hierarchies and page order, allowing you to organize your content by creating children and grandchildren.

You can still upload photos and other media. You can also code page templates into your theme to allow the user admin to choose different layouts for the page to be displayed.

Comments

Comments are the backbone of any blog. The idea, of course, is to get more users to the website and hopefully engage them to comment on what was written or created. Comments are typically created by visiting users via a form on your post or page.

Comments can be turned on or off on a per-post or per-page basis. You can also create site-wide settings that allow you to better filter comments and prevent spam from showing up (we'll talk more about this in the Settings and Administration section of this chapter).

In the Comments section of the admin you can see all the comments that have been left on the site. You can toggle approval for each comment, essentially showing or hiding the content on the front end of your website. You can also delete comments or mark them as spam. Make sure you're using an anti-spam plugin like Akismet. Marking comments as spam will help Akismet perform better for everyone in the future.

Be prepared for a great deal of spam—it's inevitable and it's the reason why Akismet comes installed by default with every new WordPress install.

Expanding Inherent Functionality and Design

WordPress comes with out-of-the-box features, functions, and presentation. However, you're not stuck with them.

Appearance

As we come farther down the menu we arrive at the Appearance section. Everything from here down on the menu can be accessed only by users with admin-level access. Here you can change themes, add or modify widgets, create menus, and more.

In the Themes section you can see that two themes come automatically installed: Twenty Ten and Twenty Eleven. The latter is already activated.

In the theme files (which we'll learn much more about later) there's a functions.php file that has the power to change and manipulate the admin. For example, the Twenty Eleven theme adds the Theme Options, Background, and Header options to the Appearance menu. These are specific to this theme. You should be aware of what's changing based on the different themes you're activating. You can see what options a theme provides after you've activated it, under its description in the Themes section.

Installing and Activating Themes

Installing another theme can be done directly in the admin window by clicking the Install Themes tab at the top of the Themes section and uploading a .zip file of the theme or accessing the WordPress Themes Directory. You can also do this manually if you have access to the server files via FTP. Activating a theme is as simple as locating the theme you want and clicking Activate. You'll also have the option to preview the theme in a lightbox before you activate the theme.

If at any time you want to change themes or go back to a previously installed theme, you can always just reactivate it.

Widgets

Several widgets come preinstalled with WordPress but you can add more by writing or installing plugins. "Sidebars" (a term that should be changed for semantic reasons) are defined to house widgets. You can have as many sidebars as you'd like. They're defined in the functions area of your theme.

Unfortunately, sidebars are not independent of your theme, so if you change your theme your sidebars will disappear. Basically, if you take the time to implement several widgets into your site and then later change themes your widgets will not necessarily carry over to the new theme. Widgets are inherently easy to apply and this makes it easy to duplicate them in the future if need be.

The theme developer will decide how sidebars will be utilized in a theme. In most cases a sidebar occupies a smaller column to the left or right of the main content and houses widgets including (but not limited to):

- Recent posts
- Recent comments
- Popular posts
- Links
- Menus

Menus

Before menus, creating dynamic navigations was no simple task. Today developers can predefine menu locations or uses; for example, you might have the Main Nav for your header navigation or Footer Nav, which would show up in the footer.

The user admin can add pages, categories, and even custom URLs to her menu. Once the menu is created she can associate her menu with the developer's predefined location in the drop-down menu at the top left, essentially empowering the user admin to take full control of all the navigations in a theme.

Adding items to a menu is extremely simple. You can select pages and categories from the left sidebar and add them to the menu. Rearranging them is as simple as dragging and dropping. You can also create tiers or a hierarchy for drop-down menus, and so on. If you want to link to an outside site, you can add the link in the Custom Links window.

Clicking Screen Options shows you options. You can add or modify classes and descriptions, and link targets or relationships for each menu item. You can also toggle whether you want the ability to select posts or tags to add to your menus.

Editor

I recommend staying out of the Editor section. Here you can modify theme and plugin files directly in the admin. However, since you're a web designer, it's likely you have the ability to pull these files down, edit them in an integrated development environment (IDE), and upload them back to the server.

Try to avoid editing plugins and themes you didn't create. Editing plugins may give you the added functionality you're looking for, but if you ever update that plugin all your changes will be lost. If you're editing a plugin, it's best to duplicate it and modify the name so you can avoid this mistake.

And rather than editing themes, try creating children themes. You'll limit the risk of losing your changes and also be using best practices. A child theme is based on a parent theme. Once you create a child theme you can alter any file in the parent theme by duplicating it to the child theme directory. With child themes you are only modifying specific template files rather than duplicating the entire parent theme. This way you have more control of specific elements and work from an untouched parent theme. For more info on child themes go to http://wdgwp.com/child-themes.

Installing and Activating Plugins

WordPress plugins can extend your site's abilities to extraordinary levels. At the end of this book I showcase some of my favorite plugins created by some amazing WordPress developers.

Adding and removing plugins is done in a similar fashion to themes. You can manually upload themes, which we'll do in Chapter 4, "WordPress Theming Basics." You can also access the WordPress Plugin Directory and install themes right through the admin or upload a .zip file through the admin as we discussed earlier.

A word of caution: Not all WordPress developers utilize best practices and, in some cases, plugins can conflict or do harm to your site. It's important to review plugins before installing them and to get an idea of what other community members think about how they work and run on their sites.

If you install and activate a plugin and then notice a problem with your site or find that the plugin simply isn't working, start by deactivating the plugin and see if that fixes the problem. In most cases, it means that your theme doesn't support what the plugin is trying to do or you have another plugin that conflicts with the new one.

Another important thing to remember about plugins is when they were last updated or when the author last commented in the forums for that plugin. If these happened recently, it shows that the author still has an active interest in the success and advancement of the plugin.

Settings and Administration

Other parts of the WordPress Dashboard have to do with ways to manage users, access tools to manage the site, and adjust the site settings.

Users

Depending on the way a website or blog is maintained, you may need several users doing different things. There are several roles created by default in the WordPress system. You are an admin and have access to everything and are empowered to perform any action.

There are also editors, authors, contributors, and subscribers, each with different levels of access and abilities. You can learn more about WordPress roles and capabilities at **http://wdgwp.com/roles**. As a WordPress developer, you can change role capabilities or even create new roles.

By default, the first user on a new WordPress install is the admin, who has admin-level access. It's important to create a new user admin account and change the admin's role to subscriber. Since WordPress is so well-known, it's common for hackers to attempt to access websites by using the admin username and guessing a password. If you change the admin to a subscriber, then hackers attempting to infiltrate your site will have access only to basic profile information if they are successful.

User Profiles

All users have access to their profile, where they can edit their name, e-mail address, password, avatar, and more. We can build on these values to improve author pages or create more advanced user profile pages.

A username cannot be changed once added, so make users aware of this. You can also modify user preferences when browsing the WordPress admin. In addition, it's important to change your display name to something other than your username. Otherwise, if you're authoring posts as an admin, readers will know your username and may be able to guess your password to gain access to your site.

Tools

The default tools are very rudimentary but provide some decent functionality. Initially, you have the ability to import and export content. You're also given a *bookmarklet* called Press This, which makes it amazingly simple to share content on the fly. You can read more about Press This at **http://wdgwp.com/press_this.**

Importing Tools

If you're converting an existing site to WordPress or bringing content over from WordPress. com, the Import tool will make your life much easier. Originally the import tools were built into the WordPress core, but in an effort to save time and file size, the code was separated and made into a separate plugin.

Once you install the plugin (which can be done automatically once you select the content source under Import) you can import content from a variety of sites including, but not limited to, Blogger, Live Journal, Tumblr and, of course, WordPress.

Exporting Tools

Exporting your content is simple but the default setup does not provide you with a lot of options. Downloading an export of your content will save an .xml file to your computer, making it easy to import your content into another WordPress install or simply back up your site. You can choose to include, posts, pages, and other content types if applicable.

Settings

As with all other sections in WordPress, as you activate new themes and plugins you'll notice more nav items. It's common for plugins and themes to provide options to modify their settings under this section.

It's a good idea to educate user admins about this as a simple change in this section can have a huge impact throughout the site. It's possible to take down an entire site with the wrong click of a button (we'll talk more about this below).

GENERAL SETTINGS

Under the General Settings tab you'll see some basic site options. Site title and tagline are pretty straightforward. Next, you have the WordPress address and site address. By default, these are the same, but if you'd like to install WordPress in one directory and have it appear to be another you can change those settings here.

Membership is helpful to sites that want to collect user data, possibly for a newsletter or other practical use. Turning this on does attract spammers, so be wary and don't set the default role higher than subscriber unless you know what you're doing.

You can also modify the date format and time zones for your personal preferences in the admin.

WRITING SETTINGS

The writing settings let you create some basic preferences when writing in WordPress. You can also set default settings for categories and post formats. You'll see the Press This option again as well.

Below that are the options for posting via e-mail and from other applications or solutions. Posting via e-mail requires that you set up a specific e-mail address to receive your posts, otherwise all your incoming e-mails could be converted into posts.

Remote publishing is amazingly helpful if you have a tablet, smartphone, or other mobile device. You can publish content straight from these devices to your WordPress website via the WordPress mobile app.

Update services allows you to create a list of sites that should be "pinged" or alerted when new content is added to your site. If you're a professional blogger, there are several sites that accept these forms of alerts in an effort to better link to your content.

READING SETTINGS

This section houses some basic settings. Most sites utilize a home page theme that has a sliding gallery, the most recent posts, and more. However, if you'd like your users to start on a specific page you can do this via the Front Page Displays area. This essentially bypasses the home page of your theme and takes the user directly to an internal page without modifying the URL.

DISCUSSION SETTINGS

The Discussion section is probably the meatiest of all the settings in WordPress. You have a lot of options for comments and what to do when one is left on your site. You can choose to be notified, hold it for moderation, and more.

You have three basic options for your Discussion Settings:

1. Allow all comments to display on your site immediately, and rely on anti-spam software to limit the bots. You can then go back and unapprove any comments you'd rather not display. The benefit here is that it's usually less work, but it can be a public relations nightmare for companies that need to protect a brand or product.

2. Don't approve anything automatically. Instead, have everything go to a queue and you'll need to manually approve all comments before they go live. This is usually best for the aforementioned companies but does require more work.

3. Use a combination of options 1 and 2 (this is the default option). In order for a comment to appear on your site, the commenter must have had a previously approved comment, otherwise it's held in moderation until you approve it. This is helpful if you have a loyal following of users.

You can also set your notification level and some other anti-spam related settings.

MEDIA SETTINGS

For me, the media settings are the most empowering in terms of displaying site content. You can change size settings, allow for auto-embedding of content, determine where files go when they're uploaded, and more.

When you upload a photo to WordPress, it is duplicated, resized, and, if necessary, cropped. This is very helpful if you're uploading photos that may be too large for the web straight from a camera. Instead of being forced to crop and manage media content, WordPress does the work for you. Here you can set the default sizes for those images, so they'll work better when integrated into a custom theme.

PRIVACY SETTINGS

Privacy settings is the smallest section, made up of a single question that asks if you want search engines to index your site. Most search engines respect the user of robots.txt files, which are created on the server. In the robots.txt file you can tell search bots whether you want them crawling your site or not. For more info on this and search engine optimization best practices, go to http://wdgwp.com/seo.

Please be aware that changing this setting to not allow search engines to crawl your site does *not* make your site private or hidden.

PERMALINKS

Permalinks define the end of a URL after the main domain. If your website domain is http://mywordpressblog.com, the permalinks define the format of the URL after the domain. The default setting is simply an attribute and value; for example, http://mywordpressblog.com/?p=123.

Other settings are available for you, but you're also given the option to create your own custom structure. I prefer to go with /%category%/%postname%/ format, which, when applied, returns results like those shown at http://mywordpressblog.com/articles/wordpress-101. In this example, I wrote an article called "WordPress 101" and put it in the Articles category.

You also have the option to modify the slug of any post or page that changes the permalink to a certain degree. Best practices dictate that you not use uppercase letters, spaces, and certain characters, among other things.

What's Next

We've just covered the basics of any WordPress-powered website. The best way to learn your way around WordPress is to create a clean install on a local or testing server, then get in there, add content, modify settings, and mess around. Try to break then fix things. Eventually you'll get a handle on the WordPress admin.

The WordPress Codex is the best place to start learning about advanced WordPress topics, but it can also be hugely helpful to beginners. If you're looking for further details on the WordPress admin, adding content, or modifying settings, check out the basic WordPress lessons at http://wdgwp.com/lessons.

In the next chapter we are going to take a deeper look at WordPress template files used in themes. These files dictate the layout of the front end of the website. Mastering the names of these files, what functions they perform, and the hierarchy they fall into is a vital step to becoming a WordPress developer.

Dear Web Designer,

When I installed WordPress for the first time, I just about had a panic attack. The dashboard was full of terms I didn't understand and it was extremely intimidating. What I didn't understand at the time was that I needed only what I understood at that point.

Install a theme—it's not that difficult—and write a post. Tag it, pick a category, and publish. Easy, right? That was just enough to focus on for the first few months. Only after creating some real quality content did the other stuff matter. There are amazing websites with mediocre designs that effectively spread their message, but I don't know of any beautiful sites with garbage content that anyone pays attention to.

After a few months I dove into plugins and widgets. Experience has taught me that less is more as far as plugins go. If a social network doesn't bring me traffic, I get rid of its plugin. It's important to have a site that loads quickly, and having fewer plugins (or the lightest ones possible) helps increase speed.

Over the years, the back end of WordPress has become more and more user-friendly. The drag-and-drop interface has made it very accessible, but I still love getting in under the hood to play with the CSS a little and create a site that's just a bit different.

I've broken my site many times, but it's always been put back together again. Sometimes it's just a misplaced symbol that I've been able to locate after a few passes; other times I've had to hire folks to find my errors.

When I'm looking to try something new with WordPress, I go to the forums and quite often I'm led down a rabbit hole. I'll be trying to find a fix for a certain plugin and the next thing you know there's a thread about a snippet of code that does something really cool and two hours later I'm still reading the forum like it's a gossip magazine. None of this is time wasted. It's learning about what you can do, and, even if you never use the capabilities, it's good to know what's possible.

Jessica Gottlieb
jessicagottlieb.com | @jessicagottlieb

PART 2
WordPress Theming Basics

WordPress theming can take years to master. Especially since WordPress is continually growing and improving. You have to stay on your toes and remain continually aware of the new and different things happening in the industry. The goal of this section is to lay the groundwork for a good understanding of WordPress theming basics.

With a good foundation and proper comprehension of exactly how each element functions, you'll learn the more complex pieces faster and retain them better. Even if you have tinkered with WordPress theming before, it's important to go through this section with an open mind.

In the next two chapters you'll learn about the WordPress hierarchy and get an introduction in to WordPress functions, template tags, and even The Loop. A good understanding of the hierarchy is the key that will empower you to build better, more complex themes.

WordPress
Template
Hierarchy

Your WordPress site can have a very simple and straightforward design with basically the same structure, functions, and presentation on every page. Alternatively, you could use template files to create very different experiences on every page. I aim for a seamless visual experience and harness template files to introduce variations that enhance functionality. The more you customize, the more complete the experience will be.

Implementing author bios on author archive pages or category descriptions on specific category pages provides the user with a better experience and more information. Doing these right means creating custom-built template files for them.

What you're about to learn

- How WordPress decides which page template to use and when

- WordPress template hierarchy

- Best practices for URL structuring

- Specific uses for custom template files

Template Files

WordPress themes are built on specific template files. These template files are called at specific times and dictate the structure of the HTML output by combining markup with PHP functions (also known as *WordPress Calls* or *Template Tags*). There are many different template files, which we'll go through shortly. At a minimum, a theme must have a style.css and an index.php file to function.

> ██▉ **NOTE**
>
> While your theme can function with only an index.php file and a style.css file, this is not a best practice. In fact, WordPress has deprecated this function and throws errors in "debug mode." In the future it may not be supported, so you should always build out your themes with all necessary template files.

The style.css file not only houses the styles for your theme, but at the top of the document, commented out code is also used to name your theme, among other things. The index.php file is the default template page for every section of a WordPress site. It's possible, with the use of conditionals, to have an entire theme work from a single index.php template file.

When I developed my first WordPress theme, I found it easy to understand the system by utilizing a single template file for the entire site. This is obviously not a best practice, but it helps you create a foundation in Theming and gives you a better understanding of when elements are called.

In my first theme, the index.php file contained the HTML structure for the whole site. It included a basic loop. The loop (which grabs and displays the content for the page we're on) was built to display a single post, page, or loop through archives or recent posts for the home page. A simple conditional tested whether we were on a single post, to display the comments. Another conditional said if we were not on a single post or page, then an excerpt of the content would be displayed; otherwise, the entire content area would be displayed. Other than that the entire site was structurally the same.

This is a very high-level overview of one way to build a theme. We'll cover all the aspects of theming as we progress through this book. The rest of this chapter will give you what you need to build a strong foundation in WordPress Theming and template page creation. It's vital that you read this chapter thoroughly.

Template Page Selection

As we move through this book and you build out your theme, you'll learn that the visitor's location on your site dictates what template pages are used to display content. If a visitor is on http://domain.com, the home page template is used, whereas http://domain.com/category/articles (assuming you've modified your permalinks structure) requires the articles category template file.

When a visitor goes to a WordPress site, mod_rewrite changes the ugly, variable-heavy URL into a neat, directory-based URL. (You can learn more about mod_rewrite at **http://wdgwp.com/mod_rewrite**.) For example, if you're visiting a post called "J2 Theme" that's in the Projects category, your URL might be http://domain.com/projects/j2-theme. But at its core, the WordPress URL is actually something like http://domain.com/?p=13.

BEST PRACTICE

The permalink settings in the admin give you control over the structure of your URLs. For semantic URLs that are better for search engine optimization (SEO) and reading, you can create a custom permalink structure. My default /%category%/%postname%/ produces an easily read and SEO-friendly URL structure.

WordPress uses the visitor's location on the site to determine that he is viewing a single post. From there WordPress looks first for very specific page templates, then default templates, all the way back to index.php, if it does not find any template that is more specific.

Template Hierarchy

Now let's look at some basic template hierarchy concepts. For an in-depth examination of the hierarchy and a list of all the template page names, visit **http://wdgwp.com/template_hierarchy**. The template hierarchy creates the structure needed to build template pages. The basic template files are:

- index.php—the default page template often used for the home page

- single.php—individual posts or nonhierarchical custom post types

- page.php—individual pages or hierarchical custom post types

- archives.php—archives like posts by date, category, or author

A simple WordPress theme will implement these template files to give you greater control over the structure and content of a page. For example, the categories page will likely list a lot of posts with blurbs of content and have pagination at the bottom to go through all the content. A single post or a short blurb wouldn't need pagination, but it would need the commenting function. While we could perform all this in the index.php with conditionals, it would quickly become a huge mess.

Part of your job as the developer is to make decisions about when to create separate page templates to accomplish functional goals. The great thing about the template hierarchy is that you can drill all the way down to specific post types, archives, and more.

Let's say a visitor goes to the Projects category via http://domain.com/category/projects. WordPress follows a path looking for the existence of a template file it can use to serve up content and markup structure:

1. category-projects.php or category-2.php
   (assuming the projects category has an id of 2)

2. category.php

3. archives.php

4. index.php

In this case, WordPress starts by looking for a file called category-projects.php, which would be used specifically for the Projects category. When it can't find that file, it moves on to category.php, which is used specifically for categories. Next, it looks for archive.php, which is used for categories, tags, dates, authors, and so on. Finally, it defaults to index.php.

As you can see, WordPress starts looking for very specific template files then works its way back to index.php, getting broader and broader each time. For a diagram of all the template filenames and the order in which they're delivered, go to **http://wdgwp.com/hierarchy-diagram**. Some page locations have only one choice. For example, the Search Results page starts with search.php then defaults to index.php.

When you're looking at the diagram note, it reads left to right. So your most specific template files are on the left and index.php, the fail-safe, is all the way on the right. It's important to read through this diagram so you have an understanding of all the template pages you can create.

Most WordPress developers, when starting out, might be unaware that front-page.php, home.php, date.php, or attachment.php even exist. Once you see these in the diagram, a lightbulb should go off in your head alerting you to further ways you can control your theme.

Uses for Specific Template Files

There are so many reasons and ways to customize your template files. This book can't cover them all, but here are a few examples. Once you have control of the markup and PHP in the template, you can do anything you want.

Home Page

Your default index.php might be really simple, but your home page can be out-of-the-box unique. In this case, you don't want WordPress to default back to your home page to display content you didn't compensate for. So, you can create home.php or front-page.php (depending on your site configuration), which lets you separate the home page from the rest of the theme.

Authors

You might be running a blog that has several authors who create large amounts of content. The author pages can default to the archive.php or index.php template file. Alternatively, you can create an author.php template file to change the layout of the pages for authors. This way it's easier to add author information at the top of the page. There you can put the author's bio, Gravatar, URL, and more.

You can take it a step further and create author-johndoe.php, allowing you to control the design of the page for this specific author (after the hyphen put the "nicename" of the desired author). Maybe John Doe is the head of the blog or the lead author. This way you can provide him with a larger bio section, more links, or even change the background image of the site.

Custom Post Types

If you're doing any work with custom post types, you'll probably want to control the display of that content in a custom format. In this case, you can create single-product.php (if product were the name of the custom post type). Often this template file is designed specifically for your custom post type, whether it's a simple featured image or a complex list of metadata for company locations.

What's Next

Being able to control the design of each page, category, or post type at a granular level is really powerful. The great thing about everything you just learned is that WordPress does the majority of the work. You need only create the template file; once it exists, WordPress will use it wherever it's appropriate. In the next chapter, you'll actually get to write some code when we develop a very basic WordPress Theme.

WordPress
Theming Basics

4

I'm often surprised to learn how complicated it is to work with other CMSs. As we've seen, WordPress has a very low barrier to entry, which means you can learn the system and build themes faster and more efficiently. At this point you know your HTML, CSS, and probably JavaScript. The only difference between a static website and a WordPress theme is stripping away that static content and replacing it with dynamic CMS calls.

I'm also surprised to meet web designers working in WordPress who don't realize they are writing PHP. PHP is the server-side web development language behind WordPress. Even if you're well aware of what it does and how it works, you probably haven't written much PHP. Well, guess what? Today we're diving right in.

What you're about to learn

- WordPress theme requirements

- Theming basics

- Dynamic header calls

- Menu nav creation

- Content formatting

Five-Minute Theme Build

You need only two template files (index.php and style.css) to create a functional WordPress theme. Index.php is used to make WordPress calls to display content, while the style.css file houses site styles and defines the theme name, description, and other details. In this chapter, we'll create a very simple WordPress theme using some basic required files.

> **■■■ NOTE**
>
> While you can technically create a WordPress theme with just two files, it is not recommended. In fact, in the future other files like header.php, footer.php, and comments.php will be required.

Theme Requirements and Declarations

Let's start by creating a blank style.css file and putting it in the theme folder. Name your theme folder something simple yet unique and don't use any spaces, numbers, or special characters.

```
🗀 my-basic-theme
    └─── style.css
```

If you haven't installed a local server application yet, that's OK. For now we're just doing some very basic programming. However, to test the theme you'll need to install WordPress somewhere.

> **BEST PRACTICE**
>
> No two themes can have the same declaration details, as this will cause conflicts in the WordPress admin. Unique naming conventions are paramount.

The absolute first thing in the style.css file has to be the theme declarations, which are commented out to prevent interaction with actual site styles. This section is called the "stylesheet header." Below is the stylesheet header for our first basic theme. Be aware that changing this information on an activated theme is likely to cause a slight glitch and require reactivation.

```
/*
Theme Name: My Basic Theme
Theme URI: http://webdesignerguidetowordpress.com/
Description: My first WordPress theme
Author: Jesse Friedman
Author URI: http://jesserfriedman.com/
Version: 1.0

Tags:

License:
License URI:

General comments (optional).
*/
```

Feel free to replace the text in maroon with your information. The black text must be absolutely perfect and mirror what you see above. Changing "Theme Name:" to "ThemeName:" will result in a broken theme.

The next step would be to add site styles, but we're building a very basic theme so we won't be inputting any styles at the moment.

We don't actually have to add anything to the index.php file right now. Let's start by simply creating a blank file and placing it in the same theme folder as the style.css file above:

```
📁 my-basic-theme
    ─── style.css
    ─── index.php
```

Theme Installation and Activation

That's it! You've created a WordPress theme. Now let's install it by adding it to the themes folder on the server. Upload your files via FTP to the wp-content/themes directory on the server. You can avoid FTP by "zipping" up the theme and uploading it under the "Add New" tab in Appearance and Themes.

Once the theme is uploaded you can go to Appearance → Themes and see the theme ready and awaiting activation. It's missing a thumbnail, but since we don't really have anything to take a screenshot of at the moment, we can leave it blank. We will cover how to add a screenshot to your finished theme in Chapter 19, "Test and Launch." You'll also notice that all the theme details from the stylesheet header are there, too.

Activate the theme and then navigate to the front of the website. You'll see a very simple site, with no content. Who says we shouldn't be proud of a plain white screen?

The Next Half Hour

The theme is still quite bare but that's OK—we're going to add to it right now. By default, all WordPress installs start with one post, one category, one page, and one comment. It makes sense at this point to go in and add a few extra pages, posts, and other content to make it easier to test the theme's functionality.

Now that we have some content to work with, let's identify some WordPress theme basics. A typical website, WordPress–powered or not, will have branding, navigation, and site content, and all of these will be written in HTML.

If you head over to http://wdgwp.com/downloads you can download a very simple HTML file that has some basic markup and content we can use to create our theme. Copy and paste this file's contents into the index.php.

> ■■■ **NOTE**
>
> Anytime you edit the index.php or any other template files, you'll have to upload them to the server unless you're working locally. That's one benefit of running a local server application.

There's no need to reactivate the theme each time you change the template files. Refreshing the page will show your changes. Now that you've uploaded the index.php, let's visit the front of the site. You'll see the content in place (remember, it won't be pretty just yet). Technically, we have a working web page at this point, but we still haven't made anything dynamic.

The file has elements you're familiar with: title, navigation list, headings, and text within HTML tags. Next we'll replace the content, such as "Jesse Friedman | Developer," with dynamic PHP calls.

So, the document title "Jesse Friedman | Developer" will be replaced with a call to display the site title and description. Again, for now this is all placeholder text. Once you replace this content with dynamic calls, the content will automatically be replaced with content from your WordPress installation.

The navigation list will be powered by a simple menu, which we'll define shortly. After that you'll see several posts displaying only the title and content with a link to the full article, all of which will be replaced by the infamous WordPress Loop.

Now that we've defined the content, we can get to work replacing it all with dynamic calls. Let's start at the top of document in the <head> section and work our way down. In the head we have to make some minor tweaks. The <title> tag defines the title of the page you're currently viewing in the browser window.

<title>

The HTML we copied from the supplied HTML document currently looks like this:

```
<title>Jesse Friedman | Developer</title>
```

The first thing to realize about converting static content to WordPress calls is that we're simply calling PHP functions that will be replaced by content. It's easy to learn WordPress calls without really having a full understanding of PHP. This is why it's easy for web designers to build WordPress themes without really knowing that they're writing PHP.

To make the title dynamic we'll delete the content between the <title> tags and replace it with the bloginfo() function.

```
<title><?php bloginfo(); ?></title>
```

Any and all PHP functions, scripts, or code in general must start and end with <?php ?>. In some cases you can get away without the closing ?> but for now let's keep it in place. The bloginfo() function requires a parameter so it knows what you're asking for. Once it receives that parameter it will "echo" it. Below is a list of parameters that bloginfo() accepts and what they will return:

```
name = Site Title
description = Site Description
admin_email = admin@example.com


url = http://example/home (however you should use home_url('/') function
        instead)
wpurl = http://example/home/wp (however you should use site_url('/') function
        instead)


stylesheet_directory = location of theme files in wp-content
stylesheet_url = http://example/home/wp/wp-content/themes/child-theme/
        style.css
template_directory = http://example/home/wp/wp-content/themes/parent-theme
template_url = http://example/home/wp/wp-content/themes/parent-theme


atom_url = http://example/home/feed/atom
rss2_url = http://example/home/feed
rss_url = http://example/home/feed/rss
pingback_url = http://example/home/wp/xmlrpc.php
rdf_url = http://example/home/feed/rdf


comments_atom_url = http://example/home/comments/feed/atom
comments_rss2_url = http://example/home/comments/feed


charset = UTF-8
html_type = text/html
language = en-US
text_direction = ltr
version = 3.1
```

Now all we have to do is enter the parameter and we'll be done. The parameter goes between the parentheses in single quotes.

```
<title><?php bloginfo( 'name' ); ?></title>
```

The above code displays the site name set in the General Settings section of the WordPress admin.

> ### ■■■ NOTE
>
> In PHP "echo" refers to outputting content so it's visible by a user on the screen. It simply prints the content wherever the echo is called, so it's still your job to place it between HTML tags for proper formatting.
>
> You can read more about the bloginfo() function and learn all the possible parameters at http://wdgwp.com/bloginfo. As we continue through this book you'll get the hang of using WordPress/PHP functions and parameters.

Let's hop over to the front end of the site and refresh it. The title in the browser window will now mirror what you've entered into the settings.

\<style>

The next thing to do is link the stylesheet in the header. Since the theme can be used on any domain, don't try to link to the stylesheet through an absolute link. Instead, replace its location with a WordPress call like we did above. Currently, the style.css call looks like this:

```
<link rel="stylesheet" type="text/css" href="style.css" >
```

All you need to do is replace the text in the href=" " with the call to the stylesheet. Since every theme requires a style.css file, you can link to it directly using <?php bloginfo('stylesheet_url'); ?>. If you want to link to additional stylesheets, JavaScript, or other files in the theme, you can use <?php bloginfo('stylesheet_directory'); ?> followed by the location and name of the file in the theme:

```
<link rel="stylesheet" type="text/css" href="<?php bloginfo( 'stylesheet_url'
    ); ?>" >
```

\<header>

In the body there are a few elements that need replacing. Again, this results in a very simple theme, so we don't have sidebars or even a footer in this example. A quick glance at the static content shows that we have to replace the site name in the <header> → <h1> along with the <nav> with a dynamic menu. Following that we have the ten most recent posts, each in its own <article>.

Below is the static content used in the <header>:

```
<header>
  <h1>Jesse Friedman | Developer</h1>
  <nav>
    <ul>
      <li><a href="">Home</a></li>
      <li><a href="">About Us</a></li>
      <li><a href="">Services</a></li>
      <li><a href="">Portfolio</a></li>
      <li><a href="">Contact Us</a></li>
    </ul>
  </nav>
</header>
```

Let's start by replacing the text within the <h1> with dynamic calls as we did above. The first half uses the 'name' parameter and the second half of the <h1> is replaced with the site 'description.' At this point you should be getting used to replacing HTML static content with dynamic calls. It's a very straightforward process—don't let it scare you.

```
<header>
  <h1><?php bloginfo( 'name' ); ?> | <?php bloginfo( 'description' ); ?></h1>
  <nav>
    <ul>
      <li><a href="">Home</a></li>
      <li><a href="">About Us</a></li>
      <li><a href="">Services</a></li>
      <li><a href="">Portfolio</a></li>
      <li><a href="">Contact Us</a></li>
    </ul>
  </nav>
</header>
```

Next, we'll call a menu by its name to replace the list of navigational items. There are lots of parameters you can use to customize this section, but for this example let's keep it simple.

Menus

The one caveat with menus is that you have to turn them on. To do this, we'll have to deviate from our index.php file and create a functions.php file. The functions.php file lives in the theme in the same directory as the index.php and style.css. This is important: As with many template files, they must reside in the main theme directory.

Put the code below in your functions.php file.

```php
<?php register_nav_menus(); ?>
```

Once you've implemented this code you'll see menus in the Appearance section in the admin. If you haven't already, go into menus and create a new navigation menu. Call it "Main Nav," add some pages to it, and save it.

Now we'll replace the <ul> with a function to call the menu by name. Later in the book we'll look at what this means in greater detail, but for now, just know that we're calling wp_nav_menu() function and passing it an array of parameters, in this case, the menu name.

```html
<header>
  <h1><?php bloginfo( 'name' ); ?> | <?php bloginfo( 'description' );?> </h1>
  <nav>
    <ul>
      <?php wp_nav_menu( array( 'menu' => 'Main Nav' ) ); ?>
    </ul>
  </nav>
</header>
```

The above code replaces the static <header> content with dynamic content. Go into General Settings and Menus, change the content, rearrange some nav items, and get used to seeing the content change dynamically.

The Loop

The Loop is one of the more complex elements to learn, but fear not—we'll cover it in detail now. If you take a look at the static content, you can see that the same structure is repeated over and over: opening tags, title, content, closing tags. In other words, the HTML tags for each post are exactly the same, the only difference is the *content*.

```html
<article>
  <h2><a href="" title=""><!-- title --></a></h2>
  <p><!-- content --></p>
</article>
```

So, instead of a repetitive list of umpteen posts with the same structure, our template will have one loop that presents the content dynamically.

The Loop is widely known among WordPress developers as the engine behind WordPress blogs (http://wdgwp.com/loop). It runs through the markup structure, template tags, and PHP code for every available post (based on your location in a site) and formats and displays them. Any HTML or PHP placed inside the loop is repeated instead of duplicated (included) as many times as the loop runs. In most places, The Loop lists up to ten posts, but this can be changed in the reading settings or in a more advanced solution right in The Loop (we'll discuss this further later on).

For now, think of The Loop as a PHP *while* loop (which it is) that calls functions along the way. If you're on the home page, it will display the ten most recent posts in the blog. If you're on a category page, it will simply display the ten most recent posts from that category. While what is being displayed changes, The Loop itself does not, because the visitor's location, or better yet the URL, dictates what will be shown.

Here's a look at a basic WordPress loop:

```
<?php if ( have_posts() ) : while ( have_posts() ) : the_post(); ?>
  <!-- content here -->
<?php endwhile; else: ?>
      <p><?php _e( 'Sorry, no posts matched your criteria.' ); ?></p>
<?php endif; ?>
```

Let's break this down:

<?php if(have_posts()) is utilizing a simple PHP if statement to test whether the have_posts() function will return a value. If it does, then we know we have posts and we move on.

: while(have_posts()) initiates the PHP while loop using the number returned by the have_posts() function. So if the have_posts() function returns the number 10, then the loop will run ten times. Finally, we call the the_post() function, which retrieves the post data and other things.

The PHP while loop loops all the content and calls all the functions we place inside it. After that we end the loop with <?php endwhile; then call the else: ?> statement, which gives us an opportunity to do something if we don't have any posts to display.

In this case, the else statement simply echoes, "Sorry, no posts matched your criteria."

■■■ **NOTE**

The _e(); function echoes its parameter passed through the translation filters. Read more about _e() at http://wdgwp.com/_e.

Now that we've broken down The Loop, let's put it back together. We'll start by replacing `<!-- content here -->` with static HTML content as seen below:

```php
<?php if ( have_posts() ) : while ( have_posts() ) : the_post(); ?>
  <article>
    <h2><a href="<?php the_permalink(); ?>" title="">This is an Article
        Title</a></h2>
    <p>Lorem ipsum dolor sit amet, consectetur adipiscing elit. Morbi nulla
        nisi, adipiscing eu laoreet vitae, venenatis vitae velit. Phasellus
        euismod dapibus velit in laoreet. Vivamus ornare justo vehicula felis
        scelerisque non aliquam nisl semper. Curabitur nisl mauris, posuere
        sed imperdiet vel, cursus id dolor. Suspendisse varius consequat
        lorem ac luctus. Maecenas consectetur neque at turpis elementum vitae
        eleifend sem blandit. Nullam auctor, risus nec porta lacinia, ante
        sapien bibendum massa, a semper tortor odio in nunc.</p>
  </article>
<?php endwhile; else: ?>
    <p><?php _e( 'Sorry, no posts matched your criteria.' ); ?></p>
  <?php endif; ?>
```

Now let's replace the static content with WordPress calls, starting with the content within the <h2>:

```php
<h2><a href="" title=" "><?php the_title(); ?></a></h2>
```

The first step was to replace the article title with the_title();. This function displays the post title that we're currently looping through. Next we'll link to the article using the the_permalink(); function:

```php
<h2><a href="<?php the_permalink(); ?>" title=""><?php the_title(); ?></a>
    </h2>
```

We also need to input something in the title attribute of the <a>. I like to use a mix of static content with the post title. Here I want the title to be "For More Info on <!-- article title --> Click Here":

```php
<h2><a href="<?php the_permalink(); ?>" title="For More Info on
    <?php the_title_attribute(); ?>"><?php the_title(); ?></a></h2>
```

The last thing to do is call the article content. Currently, we're using a static <p> to house the content. In all likelihood, the content area will be made up of all sorts of content and HTML tags, including images and videos. Anything we put into the content editor will be displayed here when we call the the_content() function:

```php
<?php if ( have_posts() ) : while ( have_posts() ) : the_post(); ?>
  <article>
    <h2><a href="<?php the_permalink(); ?>" title="For More Info on <?php
        the_title_attribute(); ?>"><?php the_title(); ?></a></h2>
    <?php the_content(); ?>
</article>
<?php endwhile; else: ?>
      <p><?php _e( 'Sorry, no posts matched your criteria.' ); ?></p>
  <?php endif; ?>
```

That's it! We've completed our loop and our theme is now functioning and dynamic. The index.php should now look like exactly like this:

```php
<!DOCTYPE html>
<html lang="en">
<head>
  <title><?php bloginfo(); ?></title>
<meta http-equiv="Content-Type" content="text/html; charset=UTF-8">
        <link rel="stylesheet" type="text/css" href="<?php bloginfo(
        'stylesheet_url' ); ?>" >
  </head>
<body>
<header>
  <h1><?php bloginfo( 'name' ); ?> | <?php bloginfo( 'description' ); ?> </h1>
  <nav>
    <ul>
      <?php wp_nav_menu( array(' menu' => 'Main Nav' ) ); ?>
    </ul>
  </nav>
</header>
  <section>
  </section>
<?php if ( have_posts() ) : while ( have_posts() ) : the_post(); ?>
  <article>
    <h2><a href="<?php the_permalink(); ?>" title="For More Info on <?php
        the_title_attribute(); ?>"><?php the_title(); ?></a></h2>
    <?php the_content(); ?>
```

continues on next page

```
  </article>
<?php endwhile; else: ?>
      <p><?php _e( 'Sorry, no posts matched your criteria.' ); ?></p>
  <?php endif; ?>
    </section>
</body>
</html>
```

Once you understand what each WordPress call does, you can make more sense of the above code. At that point, you're like Neo from *The Matrix*, seeing Matrix code rather than people. This is a very clean and easy-to-read template, and the beauty of The Loop is that it displays the right content for each and every page you're currently viewing. Don't believe me? Start navigating your site—you'll see the content change based on the URL and the index.php template page will power everything, whether you're on the home page, a single post, or even on a Search Results page.

Let's take a break. In the next chapter, it'll be time to buckle up because this was the easy stuff.

What's Next

In the next chapter, we are going to take an in-depth look at all the template design and development files we'll be using for our theme. Instead of working with functions completely out of context, the following chapter starts us down a path of building out a complete theme from beginning to end.

Dear WordPress Pupil,

At Big Sea, we work with businesses big and small for which WordPress is an ideal content management solution. We've established the following processes to help our clients make the most of their websites:

1. During the wireframing process, we indicate which sections of the site will be editable through WordPress, so clients don't assume they can change *everything*. We use color-differentiation in our wireframes to show exactly what they'll be able to change later.

2. We use custom post types liberally. Before WP version 3, we had to direct our clients to use categories and tags—or worse, plugins—to create content like employee profiles, testimonials, or locations. Now, we set up simple custom post types with appropriate names and our clients know exactly where to go to edit their Employees or Locations information.

3. We use Mark Jaquith's WP Help plugin to provide screencasts and documentation. This simple plugin creates a custom post type that displays a Publishing Help tab under the Dashboard in the WordPress admin. We create short screencasts to walk through any custom features. We upload them to our Vimeo+ account and embed them in a post in the Publishing Help. This provides access to that refresher anytime the client needs it.

4. We record "general" screencasts that we can reuse for all clients. These cover basics like creating new posts, editing content in the visual editor, setting a featured image, and even best blogging practices.

5. We include documentation and a one-hour walk-through in every project proposal. We do the walk-through when the system is about 90 percent done, so the client can add content while we finish the design details that come with filling out the site's actual content.

These steps take a little time up-front, but they save time, hassle, and frustration in the end. Arm your clients with as much help as you can, so they actually use their websites instead of letting them sit stagnant.

Andi Graham
bigseadesign.com | @BigSea

PART 3
Advanced WordPress Theming

This part of the book covers the most in-depth and detailed theming and coding examples. We will go through the steps of constructing a theme from beginning to end. You'll learn how to create template files, utilize WordPress calls, write conditionals, and more.

A WordPress theme can be built in many different ways and for many different purposes. It's important for you to understand the reasons why we write specific code the way we do, or why certain files are used to power some pages and not others. Once we cover these advanced theming techniques, you'll have a hard greater understanding of the WordPress API and theming in general.

Learning how to build dynamically-powered websites is no small undertaking. Even though this is the largest part in the book, it's important to understand that this is only a small part of your journey to becoming a WordPress master.

Our First WordPress Website

5

In the preceding four chapters we covered WordPress basics. From this point on, we'll build on those skills while developing a theme. The J2 WordPress theme was designed specifically for this book to cover the most vital aspects of WordPress theming.

What you're about to learn

- Our plan for theme development

- Theme design best practices

- How to differentiate between content and how it will be powered

- Basic template file and site architecture planning

Design Recognition

Before we jump in, I'd like to take a moment to thank Jeff Golenski. Jeff is an extremely talented web and user-experience designer who graciously volunteered his time to design this sample site for us. Let's raise our glasses to Jeff and thank him for his time and talent. Wait, you're not drinking? That's all right, I'll wait for you to pour yourself something, I'm not going anywhere...

A Note About Jeff Golenski

As a freelance designer and developer, Jeff has worked with numerous organizations in southeastern New England (**Figure 5.1**). As the senior designer at Slocum Design Studio, Jeff oversaw and contributed to identity design, print design, and web interface design, to name just a few. He also worked as a front-end web developer at Schwadesign, Inc. Today he's a web designer and developer at Astonish, working on creating the perfect link between design and functionality using the latest standards and techniques.

FIGURE 5.1 Jeff Golenski, designer of the J2 Theme. Jeff spends most of his time designing and developing WordPress themes, which makes him a perfect contributor to this book.

Steps in Theme Development

As I discussed in Chapter 1, "WordPress," when I build a WordPress theme I usually start with site architecture, then move on to wireframing, design, front-end development, and, finally, theme conversion. Jeff Golenski and I completed the first four of these steps and in the next few chapters we'll walk you through them. This way we can focus on the most important elements and get straight into WordPress theming.

The first step is to go to **http://wdgwp.com/downloads** to download the necessary page templates. When you arrive at the site, you'll notice that the design in place is actually the one we're building. This is a good opportunity for you to navigate the site and get an idea of how the theme will function when we're done building it.

On the download page are the basic theme files we used in Chapter 4, "WordPress Theming Basics," the J2 Design FED and the J2 Theme. For now you want to download the J2 Design FED files (FED stands for Front-End Development). If you're interested, you can download the J2 Theme as well. This is the finished theme and you're welcome to reverse engineer it if you prefer to work that way.

The next steps will be as follows:

1. Install WordPress and fill the site with content (if you haven't already)

2. Review the J2 Design files to better understand the theme makeup and functionality

3. Understand the folder structure and call template files accordingly

4. Replace static content with WordPress calls

5. Create page templates and post formats

6. Test and deploy the theme

Design FED Files

In Chapter 3, "WordPress Template Hierarchy," we went over the files and template hierarchy required to create a functioning WordPress theme. When you download the J2 Design files, you'll see all the template pages necessary to make this theme work. They're labeled correctly and ready to go. If you want to, go ahead and activate the theme.

Just because we can activate the theme doesn't mean our work is done, however. All it means is that the template pages are properly formatted, the CSS coding is set up correctly, and there are no errors in the code. Activating this theme will work, but it will display only static content because we haven't put in any dynamic WordPress calls.

Header, Footer, and Sidebar

Single.php, page.php, and all the other page template files require the header.php and footer.php files to work. At the beginning and end of each of these template files we'll write:

```
<?php get_header(); ?>
```

and

```
<?php get_footer(); ?>
```

These are PHP functions defined by WordPress to locate the header.php and footer.php files in your theme. Once located, the code in those files will replace the functions.

The idea here is that most sites use very similar—if not the same—headers and footers, so why duplicate them? Your goal throughout any website build should be to limit duplicate content and code when possible. If we're using the same header on every page of our theme but don't extract it from the template pages, then a single edit to the header just got duplicated many times. This will make managing edits nearly impossible and add a lot of work to the process of maintaining a site.

In the J2 Design files, the static content in the page template files is missing the header and footer. I've simply placed this HTML content in the respective header and footer PHP files. In the following chapters, we'll convert these documents into actual WordPress themes. The first step will be to pull the header and footer into these page templates. Once we do that we'll have a working website on the front end, but again with only static content.

The same goes for the sidebar.php, which houses the sidebar or, in this case, the <aside> content. Instead of having that content exist in multiple PHP files across the theme, we can pull that content out and keep it separate for easy future maintenance.

Theme Template Files

It's important to have a full understanding of the project at hand. Next we'll take an in-depth look at the design of the theme and our approach to building it. I encourage you to review the source code of the FED files and read through the developer comments. I've gone through and clearly defined the structure of the site and how all the static content will be replaced by dynamic WordPress calls.

Home Page

At first glance you'll see a nicely designed website with a clean layout and simple function-ality (**Figure 5.2**). When you take a deeper look at the design, you can start to map out the different sections of the site. The header comprises two navigations, a logo, two advertise-ments, and a search and social bar (top-right corner).

The **first nav menu** (top-left corner) is designed to house the primary navigation. As you probably guessed, these links are made up of an unordered list (<ul>) of nav items. We'll replace this entire list with a WordPress call for a menu. Menus, which we'll discuss in greater detail in Chapter 7, "Menus and Navigation," make it extremely easy for user admins to update, rearrange, and manage a site's navigation.

The **second nav menu** (light blue bar) is intended to contain the site's main blog categories. Of course, it's always up to the user admin to fill the site with content, but it's our job to try to compensate for the most common uses of our themes. This navigation will also be replaced with a call to a WordPress-powered menu.

FIGURE 5.2
Home page.

Throughout WordPress we're going to add theme support, in other words, turn on functionality. We did it with menus already. The next step will be turning on a custom header and background. By adding theme support for these sections of the admin, we make it easy for the user admin to upload an image or graphic associated with these corresponding locations or elements. The header image can be used in many different ways. In this case, we'll use it to enable the user admin to upload the logo. We'll set size limits and auto-cropping rules to make sure it fits in the header. If the user admin hasn't uploaded a logo, we'll default to the Site Title.

The two advertisements will be made up of sidebars. Unfortunately, at this moment, sidebars aren't exactly semantic terms; they're basically widgetized areas where we can drop widgets into place. We can prepopulate these areas with default widgets, then give user admins the ability to replace them as they see fit. The search form is surprisingly easy to implement and actually exists as a default widget.

The search and social bar should be generated by the existence of custom settings in the WordPress Admin. We can define our own settings and allow the user admin to save custom values, but this is a pretty complex task and beyond the scope of this book. For now, we'll hard code these elements in, but I'll also give you resources to do it right later on.

The left column is for main or featured content, while the right column is the sidebar or <aside>. The main content area starts with an image slider, then moves on to "Recent News." The right column has a newsletter signup, social nav bar, and a series of widgets for advertisements, recent posts, and more.

The image slider is made up of an image, a title, and a corresponding link. If we were covering advanced development topics, I'd make the slider a custom post type. WordPress can store and display several types of content. By default, we have posts, pages, attachments, revisions, and menus (nav). We can also define custom versions of content and decide exactly what functions that post type will support. For example, for the slider, we could have a slider post type and the word slider would appear in the left-hand nav near posts. We could also define that the slider post type will support only a title, a featured image, and a new field for a link. This will eliminate confusion for the user admin and make it easy for him to create new sliding elements on the home page.

Unfortunately, custom post types aren't simply defined in WordPress and require a great deal of custom code. I hope to cover this in greater detail in a possible follow-up book. For now, the slider's content will be generated by the existence of posts in a specific category. Later we'll also hide this category from showing in RSS feeds, search results, and other areas of the site.

The words "Recent News" are generated from the default category's title or name. The next four posts are the most recent posts from the same default category. If the user admin wants all the categories to be represented in this area, he can have the default category act as a parent to all subsequent categories. The images located here and in the slider above, as well as the thumbnails in the sidebar, will all be powered by the post's featured image. When a user admin uploads an image and sets it to be the Featured Image or Post Thumbnail, the image is automatically resized and cropped to any number of preset settings that we define. Later we can call the different sizes of featured images to display in the corresponding locations or even grab different-sized featured images based on whether the user is on a mobile device.

The **pagination** below the posts will be defined by WordPress or possibly a plugin that provides additional functionality. We'll plan for any form of pagination, including simple Next and Previous buttons, numbers, or a mix of both.

The **right-hand sidebar** will be powered by a sidebar. The featured widget area (in red, at the top of the sidebar) can be accomplished in several ways. For now, we'll simply hard code it in.

The next area of content is the footer. Current web trends showcase a lot of content in multilevel footers, and that is what we see here. The first section of the footer (with the light blue background) is defined by another sidebar. We can continue to place widgets where we like in the sections. If no widgets exist, then the light blue section of the footer simply disappears.

As discussed earlier, the social bar and now the business and copyright information should be defined by custom settings in the WordPress admin. In this case, we'll again house this information in sidebars and provide documentation to the user admin on how to best input this content into widgets.

Post

The Post template page defines the layout and structure of a single post (**Figure 5.3**). You can see immediately that the layout of this page is nearly identical to the home page with a few simple changes. While the slider is gone, there's still a large photo at the top. This photo is defined by the **featured image** in the post and, if it's set, then the image simply won't show and the content below it will shift upward. Next is the **title** of the post. Below the title is some **metadata** showcasing the date and number of comments.

Following the metadata is the **content** of the post. This area comprises everything that exists in the content editor. The editor lets you define how content will be laid out, which is why there are images floating alongside content.

FIGURE 5.3
Single page.

Next we have the **categories** and **tags** that make up the post's taxonomy. We'll simply request a list of categories and tags that this post is assigned to. Below the categories is the comments section.

Comments can sometimes be complicated. We can call the default comments template or go as far as customizing every detail of the comments area. Typically, you'll want to plan for a comment, reply comments or threads, and the actual comments form. There are several conditionals that go into the comments section, such as checking for threaded responses, determining whether users are currently logged in, and more.

Page and Full-Width Page

The Page template page looks surprisingly similar to single.php (**Figure 5.4**). In this case, there are actually only a few subtle differences. This reminds me of the game you'd find in *Highlights,* the kids' magazine, where you have to spot the differences between two images. I honestly considered having the next few paragraphs hidden at the end of the book with a "Look for answers on page..." note.

If you were any good at that game, you've already noticed the differences:

- A different-sized featured image

- Breadcrumb navigation

- A different page title design

- A tagline below the title

- No metadata showing the date or number of comments

- No taxonomy, pagination, or comments sections

Other than the differences listed above, we could simply rely on the single.php page template. If I didn't provide you with the page.php HTML document, I'd suggest duplicating single.php and making the changes outlined above by adding new classes, removing calls, and so on.

Instead, we can quickly go through the differences at a code level and create a proper page template page. Later we'll duplicate it to create a full-width page template. Page templates let us choose from layouts when creating pages. The only difference between the default page template and the full-width version is the removal of the sidebar with the extension of the main content toward the right (**Figure 5.5**).

FIGURE 5.4
Page template page.

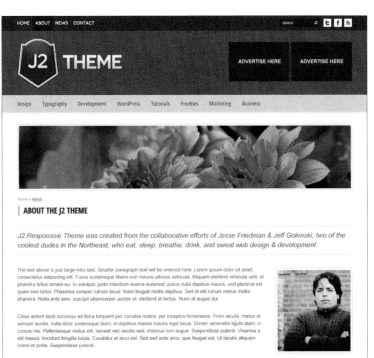

FIGURE 5.5
Full-width page
template page.

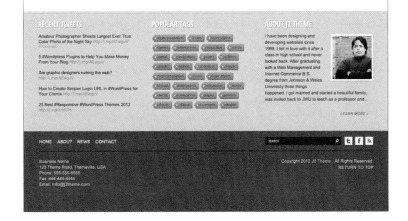

Archives and Search Pages

The Archives and Search Results template pages are nearly identical to the home page (Figure 5.6). In fact, we're only removing the slider and replacing it with a page title. The title will be very dynamic, with a few conditional statements to detect what page the user is actually on. For example, if the visitor is looking at a category called "Articles," the title would read "You are viewing the 'Articles' Archives." If, however, the visitor is on a date archive page for the month of December, it would read "You are viewing Posts from December 2011."

Upon searching the site, the Search Results page displays the results in the same fashion as the Archives page. The title grabs the search query and displays it like this: "Search Results for 'css3 tutorials.'" The only other differences from the Search Results page is the removal of the featured images and the addition of an excerpt. This way the visitor can scan the search results and find what he's looking for with ease.

What's Next

Now that you have a clear understanding of the content areas and how we'll develop them, we can get started. One quick note on page templates before we do: Our templates have an excellent layout and clearly defined content structure, but there's not much variation between the pages. You can understand why this theme would make a great learning guide. However, in the future you should feel free to change the layout however you want. You can do anything from switching up the location of the sidebar to creating a completely new layout for the theme.

Page templates add powerful functionality to your theme and give you a great deal of control over how your site is laid out. As we learned in Chapter 3, "WordPress Template Hierarchy," you can even create specific templates for specific categories or other pages of content. I encourage you to take another look at the page template hierarchy in Chapter 3. Another glance may help you better understand the concepts after reading this chapter.

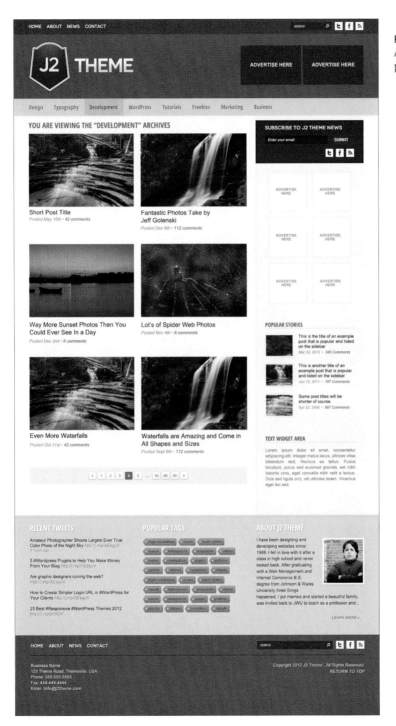

FIGURE 5.6
Archives template
page.

Theme
Foundation

Every good theme requires a good foundation. In this chapter, we'll implement a strong base for our theme by evaluating the structure of the template files, calling template files correctly, and creating our first set of WordPress hooks.

By the end of this chapter, you'll have a good understanding of how to communicate with other template files in our theme, utilize WordPress hooks for best practices, implement plugins, and extrapolate content rather than duplicate it.

What you're about to learn

- The structure of the <head> element and its importance for theming

- WordPress theme requirements

- How to link to external files in our theme

- The opening <body> tag

- How and why we maintain separate header.php and footer.php files

<head>

In this chapter, we'll spend the majority of our time in the <head></head> tags in the header. php file. The <head> tag contains a lot of calls to external files and sets the tone for the entire theme. We have to set dynamic calls for our <title> and <meta> tags, include any CSS or JavaScript files, and call a WordPress hook so plugins and other functions can add to the <head> tag as necessary.

We covered this briefly in Chapter 4, "WordPress Theming Basics," when we built our basic theme. Now we're getting a little more advanced in our coding.

<doctype> and <html>

Whether you're creating a theme for personal or client use or submitting it to the WordPress Theme Directory, it's important to declare your <doctype> correctly. In fact, it's required when submitting your theme to the directory. Our theme is built with HTML5, so our <doctype> is as follows:

```
<!DOCTYPE html>
```

The <html> tag requires us to declare our language settings, but WordPress can do this for us. Since we want to make our themes as language independent as possible, it's important to let the admin settings control the language.

Replace our <html> tag with the following code:

```
<html <?php language_attributes(); ?>>
```

Assuming you're set to US English, the above code outputs the following markup:

```
<html dir="ltr" lang="en-US">
```

<title>

In Chapter 4 we used the following code to display our dynamic page title:

```
<title><?php the_title(); ?></title>
```

This is a very basic solution, but it's actually not a best practice. Going forward, theme developers are required to use the wp_title filter to give plugins the opportunity to modify or replace the whole title. Common plugins like WordPress SEO (http://wdgwp.com/wordpress-seo) modify the page title, giving the user admin more control over SEO performance.

We're going to make only a slight change to the PHP function name in the above code. Replace the <title></title> tags in the <head> with the following:

```
<title><?php wp_title( '|' ); ?></title>
```

The only difference in the above code is that we're calling a different function: wp_title() instead of the_title(). When the function is called, we're also passing the separator parameter. The content between the quotes defines what will separate the content elements in the title. The next step is to add some code to the functions.php file to output the content of the title and return that data to the wp_title() function.

In the functions.php, the first line of code should be the opening <?php. There's no need to close this tag in the functions.php unless you plan on reopening it. As stated above, the filters will give us an opportunity to modify content before it's output in the HTML. The structure of the add_filter is 'what you're filtering (the hook),' 'the function that will perform the filtering,' 'its priority,' and 'how many parameters it accepts.' (For more information on defining filters, go to http://wdgwp.com/plugin-api-filter.)

```
add_filter( 'wp_title', 'j2theme_filter_wp_title', 10, 3 );
```

Copy the add filter function seen above into your functions.php file. We're hooking into wp_title, calling the j2theme_filter_wp_title() function, setting the priority to 10, and passing three parameters.

Now that we have our filter function in place, we actually have to filter the content. This requires that we write the j2theme_filter_wp_title() function. Copy the code below and make sure you post it **above** the add_filter function that already exists. It's important the that custom function always appears above the filter or action that calls it:

```php
function j2theme_filter_wp_title( $currenttitle, $sep, $seplocal ) {
  $site_name = get_bloginfo( 'name' );
  $full_title = $site_name . $currenttitle;

  if ( is_front_page() || is_home() ) {
    $site_desc = get_bloginfo( 'description' );
    $full_title .= ' ' . $sep . ' ' . $site_desc;
  }
  return $full_title;
}
```

The above code may appear complex, but fear not, it's actually rather simple. Let's walk through it so you'll have a complete understanding and more experience writing PHP functions:

```php
function j2theme_filter_wp_title( $currenttitle, $sep, $seplocal ) {
```

Start by defining that what follows is in fact a function. The name of the function is j2theme_filter_wp_title. We have three variables accepting parameters and their names are $currenttitle, $sep, $seplocal.

```php
$site_name = get_bloginfo( 'name' );
$full_title = $site_name . $currenttitle;
```

The next step is to define two variables, $site_name and $full_title. $site_name utilizes the bloginfo() WordPress function to get the name of the site and save it to the variable $site_name. From now on $site_name will equal the name of the site that's defined in General → Settings. The $full_title variable adds $site_name and the $currenttitle that's passed to the function. The value of $currenttitle depends on the visitor's location in the site. If the visitor is on the home page, $currenttitle will equal nothing. If she is on the About Us page, it will equal " | About Us". Notice that the spaces and the separator (which we defined earlier) are already in place.

```php
if ( is_front_page() || is_home() ) {
  $site_desc = get_bloginfo( 'description' );
  $full_title .= ' ' . $sep . ' ' . $site_desc;
}
```

The if statement that comes next is probably the most complicated part of this function. If statements are all PHP and can be written in many different ways, depending on your personal preference and the need for short code. For more information on PHP conditional statements, visit http://wdgwp.com/php-conditionals.

The if statement above asks if the visitor is on the front page or the home page, and, if so, it performs specific tasks. The is_front_page() and is_home() WordPress functions simply return either true or false. Since you can define a home page or front page in the settings, we have to test for this. The "||" is a logical operator meaning "or." In other words, if is_front_page() OR is_home() returns true (only one need be true), then we perform the code in the if statement.

Assuming those functions return true, we'll set the $site_desc variable to the site description retrieved by the get_bloginfo() function. Then we add the $site_desc to the $full_title variable. The "." means we are "adding" values together and ".=" means we are adding it to itself."

```
return $full_title;
```

The last part of the function returns the $full_title variable to the location of function call. In other words, whatever $full_title equals will be inserted between the <title></title> tags.

Below is the entire function and add_filter call to add to the functions.php file (with commenting):

```
function j2theme_filter_wp_title( $currenttitle, $sep, $seplocal ) {

    //Grab the site name
    $site_name = get_bloginfo( 'name' );

    // Add the site name after the current page title
    $full_title = $site_name . $currenttitle;

    // If we are on the front_page or homepage append the description
    if ( is_front_page() || is_home() ) {
//Grab the Site Description
        $site_desc = get_bloginfo( 'description' );

        //Append Site Description to title
        $full_title .= ' ' . $sep . ' ' . $site_desc;

    }
```

continues on next page

```
    // Return the modified title
    return $full_title;


}


    // Hook into 'wp_title'
add_filter( 'wp_title', 'j2theme_filter_wp_title', 10, 3 );
```

<meta>

Several meta tags are written into the header. Unfortunately, some of the harder things to build into a theme are meta descriptions and keywords. Especially on the home page and Archives pages there are no easy ways to create static meta descriptions. There are no meta description settings, and the tricks we might use for interior pages won't work on more dynamic pages like these. On single or page pages we can utilize the content excerpt and tags to fill the content areas of these tags.

The good news is that there are several amazing WordPress SEO plugins out there. Most of them will generate meta tags for the user admin. This is why it's so important to build themes in a way that makes it easy for user admins to incorporate plugins later.

One meta tag that WordPress can help you generate is the character set tag, which you need for compliancy. It's rather simple to implement and at this point in the book you should be able to recognize the code below. Place this code into the <head>:

```
<meta http-equiv="Content-Type" content="<?php bloginfo( 'html_type' ); ?>;
        charset=<?php bloginfo( 'charset' ); ?>">
```

Once again we call the bloginfo() WordPress function and pass it the parameter defining what we want it to return. When we do this the output HTML will be:

```
<meta http-equiv="Content-Type" content="text/html; charset=UTF-8">
```

Stylesheets and Other Template Files

Linking to external resources is easy when you're working on a static website. You know the location of your defaults.css file and it's not going anywhere. It's easy to count on that document always existing in the CSS folder in the same directory as all your HTML files. Link to it like this:

```
<link rel="stylesheet" type="text/css" media="all" href="css/default.css" />
```

The only thing that remains constant in WordPress themes when linking to a .css document is that the default file will always be named style.css and exist in the main theme folder. We can't hard code the location of the style.css file because it will likely be different in every installation of the theme. Since we can't hard code the location, we have to use a function to find it and display it every time.

Once again we rely on the bloginfo() function to output the location of the stylesheet. Copy this code into the <head>:

```
<link rel="stylesheet" type="text/css" media="all" href="<?php bloginfo(
    'stylesheet_url' ); ?>" />
```

The stylesheet_url parameter outputs the full URL needed to reference the default stylesheet. The output code below will differ for all, depending on whether we're working on this locally or on a server, whether the site is in a subdirectory, a subdomain, or in the root of the server. However, that's the beauty and the point of the code:

```
<link rel="stylesheet" type="text/css" media="all" href="http://localhost/
    j2-theme/wp-content/themes/j2-theme/style.css" />
```

Hopefully, you're asking yourself, "How do I reference other files in my theme?" This is a great point because we didn't actually put a file name into the call, so that function will only ever output the location of the default style.css file.

Linking to other files is a very similar process, but instead of calling the bloginfo() function, we're actually going to call get_template_directory_uri(). In the past it was common to use the bloginfo() function with the stylesheet_directory parameter, which would return the folder that the default stylesheet was located in. The problem with this solution is that we're not making it easy for the theme to be used as a child theme.

BEST PRACTICE

We've talked about making our themes plugin ready. Another thing to think about is making sure that they're easy to implement as **child themes**—themes that inherit the functionality of their parent. If your theme is prepared correctly, a developer can duplicate your original theme (parent) and create a child theme, which then relies on your parent theme files by default. The developer would only alter the files as needed. So if he loves your theme except for one element on the homepage, he can alter the child's homepage template and leave the parent theme files untouched. Read more about child themes at http://wdgwp.com/child-themes.

In the following code we are calling a functions.js file in the scripts folder in the theme. Outputting the template directory gets us to the theme folder. From there we need to append the location of this specific file in reference to the theme folder:

```
<script src="<?php echo get_template_directory_uri(); ?>/scripts/
    functions.js" type="text/javascript"></script>
```

It should be noted that the function get_template_directory_uri() returns the value of the location and does not automatically output it. This is why we have to put the word "echo" in front of it. Echo is not really a PHP function, but a language construct. While this may seem a little advanced, all you really need to know is that anything that follows the word "echo" will be output into code or markup. Read more about echo at http://wdgwp.com/php-echo.

The code above outputs the following markup:

```
<script src="http://localhost/j2-theme/wp-content/themes/j2-theme/scripts/
    functions.js" type="text/javascript"></script>
```

We can reuse this function call as many times as needed to gather all of the files necessary to power the site. You can use it to pull in additional stylesheets, JavaScript files, and more.

wp_head(), a WordPress Hook

The last bit of code that goes into our <head> is a WordPress function called wp_head(). This function also triggers the wp_head action hook. We discussed filter hooks previously, when we filtered the title of the page before outputting it.

An *action hook* lets developers do "something" when it's triggered. Probably the most common use of this hook is to give plugins the ability to output their own links to stylesheets or JavaScript files. The developer calls the add_action function, defines the hook (in this case, wp_head), then calls their function. This is very similar to what we did above. What follows is an example of hooking into the wp_head function:

```
<?php add_action( 'wp_head', 'your_function' ); ?>
```

We needn't concern ourselves with action hooks at the moment. However, I wanted to give you an example of its use. For now, all we have to do is add the wp_head() function just before the closing </head> tag.

At this point the header.php file should, at a minimum, look like this:

```
<!DOCTYPE html>
  <html <?php language_attributes(); ?>>

<head>
  <title><?php wp_title( '|' ); ?></title>

  <meta http-equiv="Content-Type" content="<?php bloginfo( 'html_type' ); ?>;
      charset=<?php bloginfo( 'charset' ); ?>">

  <link rel="stylesheet" type="text/css" media="all" href="<?php bloginfo(
      'stylesheet_url' ); ?>" />
    <script src="<?php echo get_template_directory_uri(); ?>/scripts/
      functions.js" type="text/javascript"></script>

  <?php wp_head(); ?>

</head>
```

<body>

The opening body tag is the last thing we'll edit in header.php in this chapter. (In the next chapter, we'll input our menus and discuss WordPress Generated Classes in greater detail. These are classes that WordPress outputs throughout the theme and site content.) Here we want to put the function body_class() into the <body> tag so WordPress can automatically generate classes based on the visitor's location and status on the site. Overwrite the <body> tag with the following code:

```
<body <?php body_class( $class ); ?>>
```

Take a moment to view the source of your site at this time. Depending on your location, whether or not you're logged in, and have the admin-bar turned on, you might see output like this:

```
<body class="home blog logged-in admin-bar">
```

You might be wondering how you can include your own classes in the body. This is another good point (you're on a roll!). While these classes help you style for many specific circum-stances, you may still want to put your own classes on the <body> tag. Fortunately, it's really easy. The body_class() function lets us pass an array of values or simply create a list in quotes.

Change the <body> tag to the following:

```
<body <?php body_class( 'container' ); ?>>
```

By adding the 'container', the output <body> tag now also has 'container' as a class.

```
<body class="home blog logged-in admin-bar container">
```

You may not use custom body classes right away, but eventually your themes will become more complex as your experience grows. At that point you'll want to do more with your themes, and body classes can take you a long way.

<footer>

Now let's jump out of header.php and into our footer.php file. Once again the theme files I've provided were correctly broken up but are completely static. We'll revisit this file as we progress through the book. The one thing we want to do at this point is input the wp_footer() function directly above the closing </body> tag. Let's pause for a second so you can guess what this function does...

Did you say action hook? Good for you! Just like the wp_head() function, we have a commonly used action hook in the footer as well. This lets developers output markup, perform functions, and more when this function is triggered.

Since you're doing so well guessing, what do you think is a common use for this hook? One thing that almost all websites do is track. Specifically, they track traffic data and metrics. Google Analytics is popular and easy to use. However, we have to put analytics code in the footer of the website. If we're creating a theme for a typical user admin, she'll likely get lost in the theme files and won't know how to input this code.

This is where the wp_footer() action hook starts working. Once we install a plugin like Google Analytics for WordPress (http://wdgwp.com/ga-wp), it hooks into the wp_footer() function and outputs the Google Analytics tracking code into the footer directly above the </body> tag.

The last few lines of your footer.php file should now look like this:

```
</footer>
  <?php wp_footer(); ?>
</body>
</html>
```

get_header(); and get_footer();

Everything we've done in this chapter will be global across our theme. The header.php and footer.php files will be pulled into all of our template pages, so it's important that we got it right.

Open index.php and you'll see the static content that's specific to the home page. We'll come back here to replace the static content with dynamic calls for content. For now, we need to code the get_header() and get_footer() functions so we can pull in our header.php and footer.php files.

It's important to make as much content and code independent of the themes template pages as possible. Anything that's duplicated across the theme should reside in its own location so you don't have to duplicate your efforts when editing things later.

In the index.php file the first line of code should be:

```php
<?php get_header(); ?>
```

This function pulls in the header.php file in the theme directory. It does the work of locating and pulling in the file's contents. The same goes for the footer. Input the following code at the bottom of the page:

```php
<?php get_footer(); ?>
```

These two functions should be duplicated as the first and last lines of code in every template page that requires a header and footer.

What's Next

Unfortunately, we don't have a lot to show for all the work we did in this chapter. But hopefully you realize that this is another step on the road to becoming a professional WordPress developer. We're implementing best practices and creating a great foundation for our theme. In the next chapter, we'll create some WordPress menus and generate our site's navigations.

Menus and Navigation

7

Before menus, dynamic navigation wasn't fun. You'd typically list pages, then categories, and rely on their hierarchies and status to dictate the menus and the existence of nav items. It wasn't easy to create custom navigation.

Today you can simply drag and drop nav items as you see fit. As a theme developer, you can define menu locations so the user admin can create menus and define where they will exist in the website. You can also customize the HTML that's output when your menu is called in the theme. Effective use of menus in your theme will benefit the user admin greatly and make for a better product.

What you're about to learn

- How menus and WordPress navigations function

- How to register menus

- Best practices for displaying menus and outputting HTML

- Site navigation management and editing

How Menus Work

As with every aspect of WordPress, there are two sides to every bit of functionality. User admins are in charge of creating the menus and filling them with nav items. You, as the developer, are in charge of defining menu locations and how the HTML will be output. Once the locations are defined, the user admin can place menus in your locations via a drop-down menu.

In Chapter 4, "WordPress Theming Basics," we pulled a menu into our basic theme using the default settings. The lack of defined menu locations in our basic theme required us to call the menu by name. This in turn requires the user admin to know the name used in the call and use it correctly. Menu locations eliminate the possibility of errors for the user admin because he can name a menu however he wants, then later just assign it to a location in the theme.

Registering a Menu Location

You should have your static J2 Theme activated, which means you can't actually see the Menus tab under Appearance because we have an empty functions.php file. As discussed in Chapter 4, you have to activate the menu function in WordPress. To save time, we'll define our menu locations now as well.

The WordPress register_nav_menu() function simultaneously defines a single menu location to be used in the theme and turns on menu functionality. (You can read more about this function at **http://wdgwp.com/register_nav_menu**.) Below is an example of this function and how we plan to use it:

```
register_nav_menu( 'your-menu-handle', 'Your Menu Label' );
```

The first parameter is the menu handle; best practices call for all lowercase letters with words separated by hyphens. The second parameter is the label, which is what the user admin will see. It's best to remain semantic and clear with your definitions.

We have three menu locations to define in our J2 Theme. **Figure 7.1** shows the main nav in the header bar at the very top, the categories listed just above the main content, and another nav in the footer.

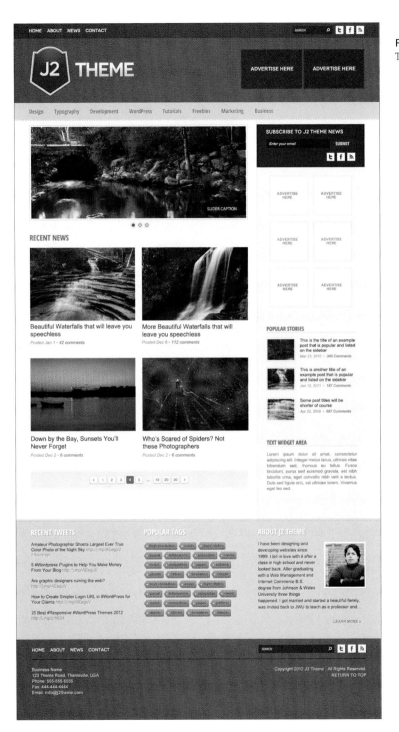

FIGURE 7.1
Theme home page.

Registering Multiple Menu Locations

The following code is a little different than what we've seen before because we're declaring several locations at once. The register_nav_menus (notice "menus" is plural this time) function lets us pass an array in order to declare multiple locations at a time. (You can read more about this function at http://wdgwp.com/register_nav_menus.)

```
register_nav_menus(
    array(
    'main-nav-header-top' => 'Main Nav, Top of Header',
    'sub-nav-header-bottom' => 'Sub Nav, Bottom of Header',
    'footer-nav' => 'Footer Menu'
    )
);
```

> **■■■ NOTE**
>
> If you're not a PHP pro, that's OK—just know that an array is a datatype with multiple values. You can see the pattern in the code and make sense of it regardless of your development background.

When you place the above code directly into the functions.php file, you'll see an immediate result in the WordPress admin. The menu functionality will be turned on and your locations will be available to fill with menus. You won't see your menu Theme Locations yet, but they'll appear once we create our first menu (Figure 7.2).

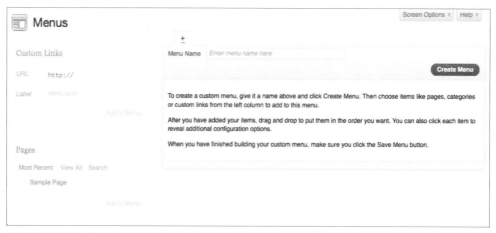

FIGURE 7.2 WordPress admin—menus.

With our menu locations in place, we can begin to appreciate the beauty of menus. They are theme independent, which means that a user admin can apply a lot of time to his menus with no risk of losing them when switching themes. The most that's required of a user admin is to go back into the Menus tab and select the menu's location from the Theme Location drop-down menu.

Creating a Menu

The next step is to create the actual navigation menu. Enter your menu name in the Menu Name field, then click the Save Menu button to the right (**Figure** 7.3). Once you do this, you'll be notified of the creation of your menu and the menu locations will appear on the left.

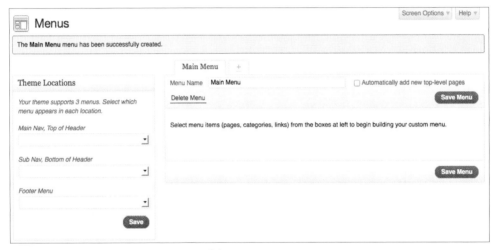

FIGURE 7.3 WordPress admin—menus with locations.

After we installed WordPress, we ran through the creation of content and built out some sample pages, posts, and categories, and even added some tags. This is all helpful now because there are several items to add to the menu. Nothing you do now will be set in stone; you can change your menus at any time, so feel free to create a temporary navigation at this point.

Once the menu exists, all you have to do is select nav items from the left to be added to the menu on the right. As you can see in **Figure** 7.4, I've selected several pages to be added to my Main Menu. I've also created a custom link, which in this case points to my Twitter page. Once I click the corresponding Add to Menu buttons these nav items will be listed on the right in my menu.

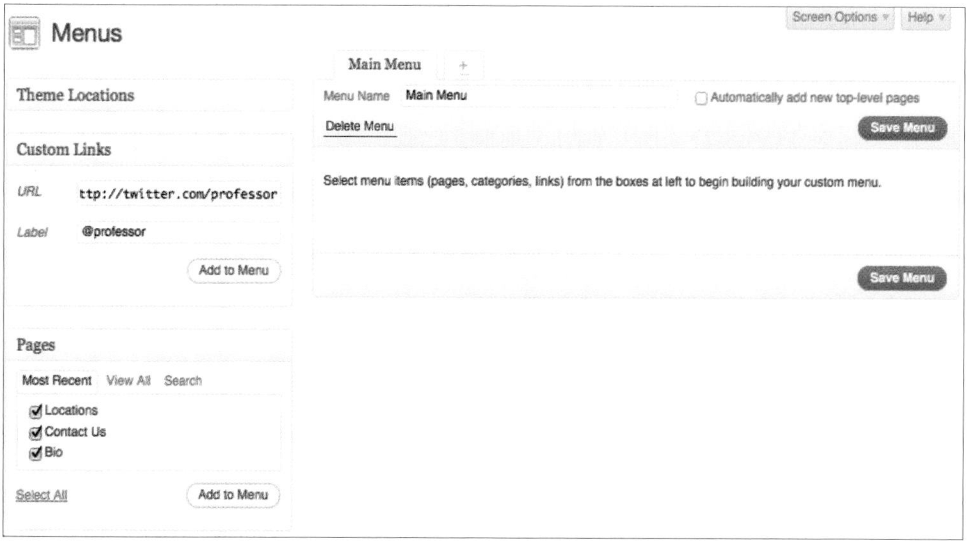

FIGURE 7.4 WordPress admin—adding nav items.

With these nav items in place you can simply drag and drop to rearrange them, as shown in Figure 7.5. You can also create nav hierarchies by placing nav items underneath one another. While you're free to create great-great-grandchildren, it's best to plan for a drop-down with no more than one additional drop-down. This would be a three-tier navigation. Later we'll define the depth in which to display the nav items.

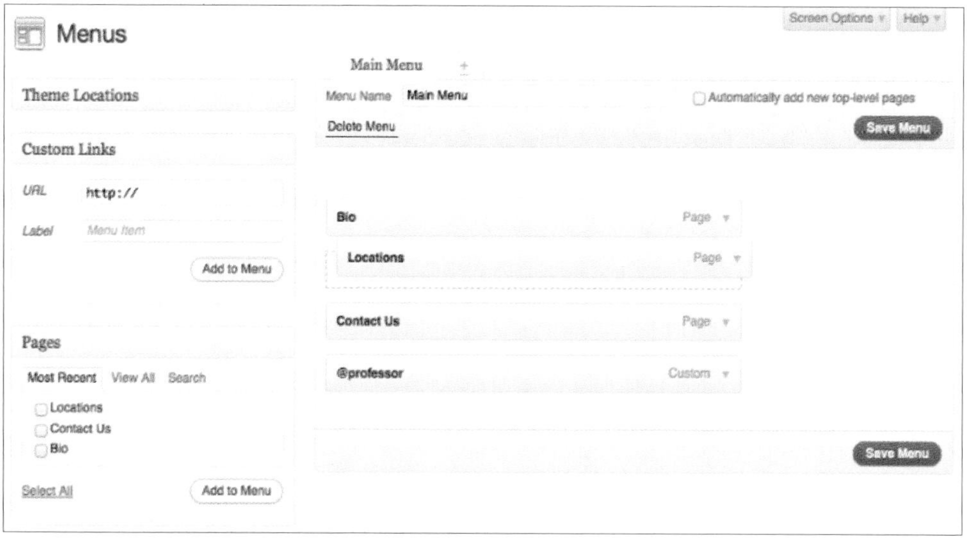

FIGURE 7.5 WordPress admin—dragging nav items.

The final step in the admin, before we actually output the HTML, is to assign menus to their respective locations. I've created an additional menu called Sub Menu and filled it with categories (Figure 7.6). Under Theme Locations you'll see the three locations we defined earlier in our functions.php file. Each location has a drop-down menu with a list of menus we created on the right.

Simply select the desired menu in the drop-down and click Save. In this example I'll be using Main Menu twice: once in the header and once in the footer. Later I can define their specific HTML elements, depth, and more, which will allow the same nav items to appear differently to the user.

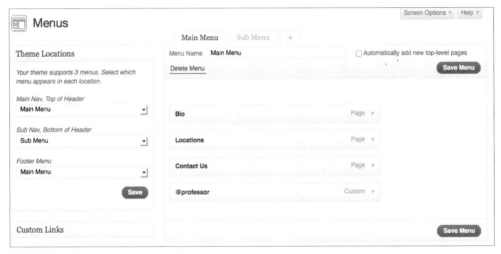

FIGURE 7.6 WordPress admin—adding theme locations.

Theme Integration

So far we've turned on menu functionality, defined menu locations, created menus, and assigned them to their locations. However, we haven't actually displayed anything on the site. The next step is to go into our theme files and replace the static HTML navigations with WordPress functions.

In the header.php file, you'll see the following code:

```
<nav id="header-main-nav" class="alignleft widecol">
    <ul>
      <li><a href="#">Home</a></li>
      <li><a href="#">About</a></li>
      <li><a href="#">News</a></li>
      <li><a href="#">Contact</a></li>
    </ul>
</nav>
```

We're going to replace this entire section of code with the wp_nav_menu() function that lets us call a specific menu, define HTML elements, classes, depth, and more. Like the register_nav_menus() function before, we're going to pass an array of parameters to it. Below is a list of all the parameters and their basic meanings. (To learn more about this function, go to http://wdgwp.com/wp_nav_menu.)

```
$defaults = array(
    'theme_location'  => 'menu,
    'menu' => ,
    'container' => 'div',
    'container_class' => 'menu-{menu slug}-container',
    'container_id'  => ,
    'menu_class'  => 'menu',
    'menu_id' => ,
    'echo'  => true,
    'fallback_cb' => 'wp_page_menu',
    'before' => ,
    'after' => ,
    'link_before'  => ,
    'link_after' => ,
    'items_wrap' => '<ul id=\"%1$s\" class=\"%2$s\">%3$s</ul>',
    'depth' => 0,
    'walker' =>
);
```

We'll only be using a few of these parameters, but I suggest that you read through them to get a better understanding of what options you have and how you can go about building better, more dynamic menus. If you feel limited by these options, you do have the ability to create what's called a custom walker, which lets you define every single aspect of the HTML output. (You can read about custom walkers at http://wdgwp.com/walker_class.)

The following code will replace the static HTML starting and ending with our <nav> tags. The first thing we're doing is defining an array called main_menu_header_top that will hold all the parameters. Then we'll call the wp_nav_menus() function and pass it to the array. This simply tells WordPress to perform the wp_nav_menus() function using the defined parameters to complete the task, and to output the HTML as we need it:

```php
<?php
    $main_menu_header_top = array(
      'theme_location' => 'main-nav-header-top',
      'container' => 'nav',
      'container_class' => 'alignleft widecol',
      'container_id' => 'header-main-nav',
      'depth' => 1
    );
?>
<?php wp_nav_menu( $main_menu_header_top ); ?>
```

Our parameters include:

- theme_location—the menu handle of the location we registered earlier

- container—the HTML element that will hold our nav

- container_class—the classes that should go on our <nav> tag

- container_id—the ID that's assigned to our <nav> tag

- depth—how many children deep our navigation should go

These parameters let us build our navigation and define the HTML output as we need it. It's all rather straightforward—just remember that with depth, if you want an unlimited number of children, set it to 0. We set our depth to 1, which means we'll have up to one child per <li>, even if the menu in the admin has several levels of children.

The output HTML maintains the same structure we had in place, except that WordPress adds its own classes. You're welcome to write a custom walker (as discussed earlier) to eliminate these extra classes if needed.

```html
<nav id="header-main-nav" class="alignleft widecol">
    <ul id="menu-main-menu" class="menu">
      <li id="menu-item-15" class="menu-item menu-item-type-post_type menu-
          item-object-page menu-item-15"><a href="http://localhost/j2-theme/
          sample-page/">Bio</a></li>
      <li id="menu-item-13" class="menu-item menu-item-type-post_type menu-
          item-object-page menu-item-13"><a href="http://localhost/j2-theme/
          locations/">Locations</a></li>
      <li id="menu-item-14" class="menu-item menu-item-type-post_type menu-
          item-object-page menu-item-14"><a href="http://localhost/j2-theme/
          contact-us/">Contact Us</a></li>
      <li id="menu-item-12" class="menu-item menu-item-type-custom menu-item-
          object-custom menu-item-12"><a href="http://twitter.com/professor">
          @professor</a></li>
    </ul>
</nav>
```

From here on the Main Nav is dynamic and will reflect any changes made in the admin. We'll be replacing the Sub Nav (just below the header and above the main content) and the Footer Nav with similar code, seen below.

SUB NAV WORDPRESS CODE

```php
<?php
    $sub_menu_header_bottom = array(
       'theme_location' => 'sub-nav-header-bottom',
       'container' => 'nav',
       'container_class' => 'clear subnav',
       'menu_class' => 'width100pad',
       'depth' => 1
    );
?>


<?php wp_nav_menu( $sub_menu_header_bottom ); ?>
```

SUB NAV OUTPUT HTML

```html
<nav class="clear subnav">
    <ul id="menu-sub-menu" class="menu">
      <li id="menu-item-16" class="menu-item menu-item-type-taxonomy menu-
        item-object-category menu-item-16"><a href="http://localhost/
        j2-theme/category/articles/">Articles</a></li>
      <li id="menu-item-17" class="menu-item menu-item-type-taxonomy menu-
        item-object-category menu-item-17"><a href="http://localhost/
        j2-theme/category/interviews/">Interviews</a></li>
      <li id="menu-item-18" class="menu-item menu-item-type-taxonomy menu-
        item-object-category menu-item-18"><a href="http://localhost/
        j2-theme/category/tutorials/">Tutorials</a></li>
    </ul>
</nav>
```

FOOTER NAV WORDPRESS CODE

```php
<?php
    $footer_nav = array(
      'theme_location' => 'footer-nav',
      'container' => 'nav',
      'container_id' => 'footer-main',
      'depth' => 1
    );
?>
<?php wp_nav_menu( $footer_nav ); ?>
```

FOOTER NAV OUTPUT HTML

```html
<nav class="menu-main-menu-container">
    <ul id="menu-main-menu-1" class="menu">
      <li class="menu-item menu-item-type-post_type menu-item-object-page
        menu-item-15"><a href="http://localhost/j2-theme/sample-page/">Bio
        </a></li>
      <li class="menu-item menu-item-type-post_type menu-item-object-
        page menu-item-13"><a href="http://localhost/j2-theme/
        locations/">Locations</a></li>
      <li class="menu-item menu-item-type-post_type menu-item-object-page
        menu-item-14"><a href="http://localhost/j2-theme/contact-us/">
        Contact Us</a></li>
```

continues on next page

```
        <li class="menu-item menu-item-type-custom menu-item-object-custom
          menu-item-12"><a href="http://twitter.com/professor">@professor
          </a></li>
      </ul>
  </nav>
```

We have now successfully replaced all static navigations with dynamic WordPress menus. You can create more menus to be used in widgets or even directly in content with *shortcodes* (we'll discuss shortcodes in later chapters).

Menus are powerful and easy to use. There are many uses for them, and I encourage you to continue investigating and experimenting with them as we continue through this theme build.

What's Next

Now that our navigations are dynamic, we're going to start building out the rest of the theme. In the next chapter, we'll identify dynamic areas in the home page and replace them with WordPress template tags.

Home Page

As we continue through the book, we'll identify specific elements of our theme that need to be converted from static content to dynamic WordPress calls. As we do this, our theme will slowly take shape and the amount of static content will be greatly reduced. This process doesn't necessarily represent the best way to build a theme: we're learning as we go, so it's a little disjointed.

The home page is a sum of content from many parts of our site. It has a header and footer, obviously. There are also two dynamic sidebars, a slider, and a most recent posts section.

What you're about to learn

- An overview of index template page best practices

- An in-depth look at The Loop

- Date formatting for HTML5 and content

- Displaying taxonomy

- How to use Template Tags

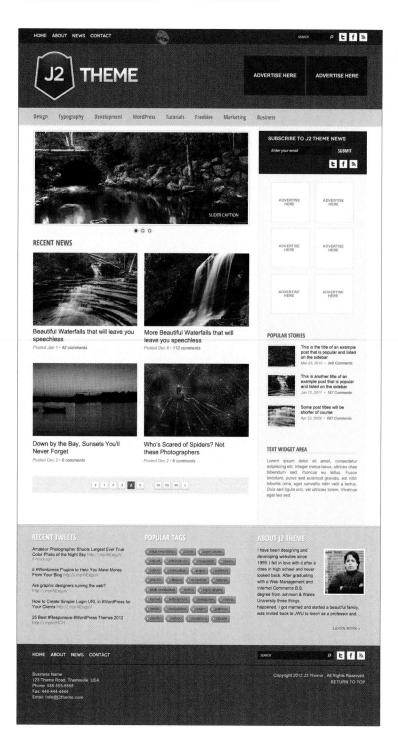

FIGURE 8.1
Home page.

Home Page Template Structure

The home page can utilize one of a few different template pages (**Figure 8.1**). Based on your settings, a home page can be a page, a list of posts, or a hybrid, which is most typical. Our home page will be based on the index.php template file. Let's start by opening the index.php template file and get to work.

get_header()

In Chapter 6, "Theme Foundation," we discussed the use of the get_header() and get_footer() action hooks. In index.php on line 1, insert the get_header() function. Make sure to copy the code below as the first line of code in this and all other template pages:

```php
<?php get_header(); ?>
```

The Slider

Most of the slider contains somewhat advanced elements that we'll address in later chapters. But let's take a quick look at the slider and its components, and why it requires an advanced solution (**Figure 8.2**).

FIGURE 8.2 Home page slider.

The HTML required to power the slider isn't overly complex. You've probably built or implemented a JavaScript–powered slideshow. The markup or HTML is usually very simple (an
example appears below). That's how it will be with our slider, but instead of handwriting the
HTML for the slider, we'll pull it all in dynamically:

```
<div id="slider">

  <a href="http://jesserfriedman.com" title="About Jesse Friedman"><img
      width="530" height="215" src="http://localhost/j2-theme/wp-content/
      uploads/2012/05/jesse-530x215.png" class="attachment-slider wp-post-
      image" alt="Image of Jesse Friedman" title="About Jesse Friedman" />

  <a href="http://worldclassdesigner.com" title="About Jeff Golenski"><img
      width="530" height="215" src="http://localhost/j2-theme/wp-content/
      uploads/2012/05/jeff-530x215.png" class="attachment-slider wp-post-
      image" alt="Image of Jeff Golenski" title="About Jeff Golenski" />
</div><!-- slider -->
```

The slider is made up of a featured image, title, and a link, all of which can be housed in a
single post. While we discussed the use of custom post types as a better solution, for now
we'll simply utilize a designated category as a holder for our slider posts.

The slider posts will set the caption of the slider with the title of the post. The image or
photo will be the post's featured image. Utilizing the featured image gives us greater control
of the size and quality of the photo and makes it easier for a user admin to implement.

BEST PRACTICE

Featured images or Post Thumbnails need to be activated in the functions.php. You should
also make it a point to define all the sizes that the featured image could be in your theme.
When you define the size of the thumbnail, you'll also give it a name so you can call the
correct image size at the right time. Since all the images are cropped upon upload and
activation of a featured image, there's no unnecessary processing time.

We'll talk specifically about the featured image in Chapter 14, "Featured Images," where we'll
activate the functionality and assign image crop sizes and names.

The next logical step would be to make the link around the caption, the URL of the post. Instead, we'll use a custom value to hold the destination of the link. We're doing this because we want to make the post independent of where the user is sent after clicking the link. This way we can link to external sites, internal pages, and specific posts, or even search results and archives. Relying on the post's URL as the link destination would require us to have content on that post at all times, plus the existence of the slider category would be known.

The last element to consider is the fact that we need to pull a limited number of posts from a specific category. The content below the slider will be generated by a generic loop, and the content and number of posts in that loop will be determined by general settings. For the slider, we'll need to do a custom query, where we define the specific category we're pulling from and the maximum number of posts we can fit into the slider. Custom queries and the generation of the slider code will be specifically addressed in Chapter 16, "WP_Query()."

The Content Area

As you can see in **Figure 8.3,** the main content area is titled "Recent News." This will change based on the content you enter into WordPress. We'll actually pull the title of the default category, which is in the user admin's hands to change. It's important to note that categories, tags, and other elements used to organize data is referred to as *taxonomy*. In the index.php template file, replace the content of the <h2> in the posts <div> with:

```php
<?php echo get_the_category_by_id( get_option( 'default_category' ) ); ?>
```

This statement has multiple functions working together to perform a single task: returning the name of the default category. The first function, get_the_category_by_id(), returns the name of the category you request by the ID. Unfortunately, we don't know the ID of the default category, so we have to request that as well. The get_option() function lets us retrieve settings from the WordPress database. We'll request the default categories ID by submitting 'default_category' as a parameter. Then we need to echo the entire statement to output the returned category name.

FIGURE 8.3 The main content area.

We could also write the above code exactly like this:

```php
<?php
  $default_cat_id = get_option( 'default_category' );
  $default_cat = get_the_category_by_id( $default_cat_id );
  echo $default_cat;
?>
```

Line 1 assigns the default categories ID to the variable $default_cat_id. Then we request the name of the default category using the get_the_category_by_id() function, passing it the variable $default_cat_id. Then we echo the variable $default_cat.

Both code examples produce the same result. The first one is shorter and leaner. The second one requires a few extra steps but may be easier to comprehend at this point. Feel free to add either into your <h2> tags.

Since we're on the home page, the posts in the content area seen in Figure 8.3 will be defined by our settings. Default WordPress settings will result in us pulling the ten most recent posts from all categories on the home page.

Later, when we build our slider, we'll define our functions.php file to exclude the slider category from all loops, search results, and archives results. We can alter the categories pulled in The Loop, which we'll talk about briefly below and learn about more in-depth in Chapter 16, "WP_Query()." To change the default number of posts throughout the entire site, the user admin can go to General Settings → Reading. In this example, I changed the number of posts to display to five.

The Loop

In Chapter 4, "WordPress Theming Basics," we covered a basic loop, and there isn't much difference between that code and what follows. Remember, The Loop is the WordPress way of grabbing all the content that belongs to the current page (defined by the visitor's current location). Since we're on the home page, The Loop will grab only the most recent posts, unless we've modified The Loop or our settings.

Remember when creating The Loop that we have to look for repeating content structures. In this case, the HTML markup for each individual post is the same:

```
<article class="halfcol alignleft">
  <img src="<!-- image url -->" alt="" title="">
  <h3><a href="<!-- post url -->" title=""><!-- title --></a></h3>
  <p>Posted <time datetime="<!-- date in datetime format -->" pubdate=
      "pubdate"><!-date --></time> &#149; <!-- number of comments --></p>
</article>
```

Everything seen above will be inside The Loop. The posts <div> that wraps the posts will not be included in The Loop because it would be duplicated for every iteration of a post. The <article> houses the post and its content, which is made up of the featured image, post title, post URL, publication date, and the number of comments. We have to post the post publication date twice, in two different formats, one for the datetime attribute and the other that will be displayed to the user between the <time></time> tags.

Starting just below the opening posts <div> we'll put the following code, starting The Loop:

```php
<?php if ( have_posts() ) : while ( have_posts() ) : the_post(); ?>
```

The above line of code is an elegant way to utilize PHP shorthand. If there are posts to serve, then perform the following iteration of HTML and PHP as many times as there are posts. The while loop will continue to go as long as the function in its parentheses returns true. So as long as there are posts, we'll be looping. The the_post() function preps the post and makes it available in the current iteration of The Loop. Without the the_post() function, much of the content would be unavailable for processing:

```html
<article class="halfcol alignleft">
  <?php the_post_thumbnail(); ?>
  <h3><a href="<?php the_permalink(); ?>" title="For More Info on <?php
      the_title_attribute(); ?>"><?php the_title(); ?></a></h3>
  <p>Posted <time datetime="<?php the_time( 'Y-m-d' ); ?>"
      pubdate="pubdate"><?php the_time( 'M n' ) ?></time> &#149; <?php
      comments_number( '0 comments', 'only 1 comment', '% comments' ); ?>
      </p>

</article>
```

The above code goes directly inside The Loop. We have a mix of HTML markup and WordPress functions, all of which will eventually make up the posts section on the home page.

> ■■■ **NOTE**
>
> Content, Template Tags, settings, taxonomies, and more can be displayed in a loop or throughout your theme. Discussing every single one would require a book as large as the WordPress Codex. For more information on The Loop and typical Template Tags used in many themes, go to http://wdgwp.com/loop.

Images in The Loop

The first function is a call to display the default post thumbnail, also known as the featured image. Since we'll go into featured images in greater detail in Chapter 14, "Featured Images," we'll table this for now. Just know that the function will return the entire <img> tag complete with src, title, and alt values (all of which are set in the post when the feature image is added):

```php
<?php the_post_thumbnail(); ?>
```

The one issue that arises now is the lack of support for featured images. Like menus, the thumbnail functionality has to be activated in the functions.php file. Take a quick second to add the following line of code in your functions.php file. This will enable theme support for featured images and prevent an error when displaying posts:

```
add_theme_support( 'post-thumbnails' );
```

The next functions are the_permalink(), the_title_attribute(), and the_title(). These functions simply output the value of the post URL and the post title, respectively. Since these functions, like many others in WordPress, automatically output the data we're requesting, there's no need to do anything other than place it where we want it. The the_title_attribute() function returns a "clean" version of the post title for use in HTML attributes. It's important to use this function in attributes to ensure that your HTML markup is compliant. You'll notice that we call the post title twice, once in the title attribute title="For More Info on <?php the_title_attribute(); ?>", and again in between the <a> tags. I've paired the post title with content in the title attribute, giving some value to the <a> tags title attribute:

```
<h3><a href="<?php the_permalink(); ?>" title="For More Info on <?php
    the_title_attribute(); ?>"><?php the_title(); ?></a></h3>
```

There are a variety of ways to reuse Template Tags and I encourage you to experiment with them in your loop. For a list of Template Tags, go to http://wdgwp.com/template_tags. Many of these are semantic in their naming conventions, so it should be easy to understand their basic functionality. You'll notice that many begin with the_ and get_. For example, the_permalink() and get_permalink(). The main difference between these functions is that the_permalink() automatically outputs the current post's URL, whereas get_permalink() returns the URL so you can assign it to a variable or perform an action on it.

Date Metadata

The post metadata comes next. We'll display the date the post was published and the number of comments currently approved on the post.

```
<p>Posted <time datetime="<?php the_time( 'Y-m-d' ); ?>" pubdate="pubdate">
    <?php the_time( 'M j' ) ?></time> &#149; <?php comments_number(
    '0 comments', 'only 1 comment', '% comments' ); ?></p>
```

While the above bit of code looks complicated, it actually uses only two Template Tags. The first is the_time(), which accepts parameters in quotes that will output the date and time in specific date and time formats. Our first call to the_time() uses the format 'Y-m-d' which translates to "2010-05-15" or a four-digit numeric year, a two-digit numeric month, and a two-digit numeric day. The content between the letters, in this case hyphens, is used to separate the data. This format is required for the datetime attribute on the <time> tags. Between the <time> tags we can format the date any way we want. I chose a simple month-day format. "M" displays the three-letter month and "j" the numeric day (without the leading zero), which outputs "Dec 31." Notice that the space between the "M" and the "j" creates a space between "Dec" and "31." There are many additional date format codes and you should review them to make sure you are displaying publication dates exactly how you want them. You can find more information on date formatting at http://wdgwp.com/format_date.

Comments

The next item we see in the template concerns the comments.

```
<?php comments_number( '0 comments', 'only 1 comment', '% comments' ); ?>
```

The comments_number() function that is seen in the <p> tag after the date performs one task amazingly well: It returns the number of comments on the current post but gives you control over how it displays. This function makes it easy to format the contextual content around the number of comments. The first parameter in quotes is what to display when there are zero comments, the second is what to display with a single comment, and the last is what to display with multiple comments. Below are some examples you could add in each place:

- "0 Comments," "No Comments," "Be the first to comment"

- "1 Comment," "Only 1 Comment," "There's only 1 comment, let's continue the conversation"

- "25 Comments," "25 comments, now we're cooking"

Anytime you want to display the number of comments use the % symbol. So, for the last parameter, '% comments' would display "25 comments" (assuming there were 25 approved comments on the post).

We have now completed the HTML markup and WordPress Calls needed in The Loop, so the next step is to close The Loop. The endwhile; statement signifies the end of The Loop while not necessarily commanding the end of it. In other words, we're saying once you're done looping, pick up here. The next statement on the same line is the continuation of the if statement with our shorthand else:. This loop all began with a PHP if statement and, in an effort to keep good form, we are offering alternative content if there are no posts to display.

```
<?php endwhile; else: ?>
  <p><?php _e( 'Sorry, no posts matched your criteria.' ); ?></p>
<?php endif; ?>
```

We finish the statement with an endif; stating, in this case, the end of The Loop.

```html
<article class="halfcol alignleft">
  <img src="http://localhost/j2-theme/wp-content/uploads/2012/05/
    thumb-example.png" alt="Our Thumbnail Image" title="Check out
    our thumbnail image">
  <h3><a href="http://localhost/j2-theme/hello-world" title="For More Info
    on Hello World">Hello World</a></h3>
  <p>Posted <time datetime="2012-05-20" pubdate="pubdate">May 20</time>
    • 0 comments</p>
</article>

<article class="halfcol alignleft">
  <img src="http://localhost/j2-theme/wp-content/uploads/2012/05/thumb-2-
    example.png" alt="Our 2nd Thumbnail Image" title="Check out our 2nd
    thumbnail image">
  <h3><a href="http://localhost/j2-theme/hello-world-again" title="For More
    Info on Hello World, Again">Hello World, Again</a></h3>
  <p>Posted <time datetime="2012-05-25" pubdate="pubdate">May 25</time>
    • 32 comments</p>
</article>

<article class="halfcol alignleft">
  <img src="http://localhost/j2-theme/wp-content/uploads/2012/06/thumb-3-
    example.png" alt="Our 3rd Thumbnail Image" title="Check out our 3rd
    thumbnail image">
  <h3><a href="http://localhost/j2-theme/hello-world-again-and-again"
    title="For More Info on Hello World, Again and Again">Hello World,
    Again and Again</a></h3>
  <p>Posted <time datetime="2012-06-07" pubdate="pubdate">Jun 7</time>
    • 1 comment </p>
</article>
```

continues on next page

```
<article class="halfcol alignleft">
  <img src="http://localhost/j2-theme/wp-content/uploads/2012/06/
    thumb-4-example.png" alt="Our 4th Thumbnail Image" title="Check out
    our 4th thumbnail image">
  <h3><a href="http://localhost/j2-theme/goodbye-world" title="For More
    Info on Goodbye World">Goodbye World</a></h3>
    <p>Posted <time datetime="2012-06-17" pubdate="pubdate">Jun 17</time>
      • 11 comments</p>
</article>
```

This is an example and would of course vary depending on the post content in WordPress.

Pagination

Since we can only show a certain number of posts on each page, we need a simple way of getting to the next page of posts. On the web, pagination is utilized in a variety of formats, from basic Previous and Next buttons to a full list of page numbers. Our pagination combines the two, with arrows, page numbers, and a break to better consolidate the beginning and end of the list of pages, as seen in **Figure 8.4**.

FIGURE 8.4 Pagination.

Pagination is required on several template pages throughout the theme. Since we want to eliminate duplication of code as much as possible, we'll replace our pagination calls with a function. Later in the book we'll write a custom function to display the pagination wherever it is called. Imagine in the future we have ten template pages using pagination. If WordPress makes an update that requires addressing or we notice a better way of writing our code, we'll have to fix the pagination code ten times. In this case, our custom function will house the code and we'll have to make the change only once.

Sidebar.php

Sidebar doesn't mean "side," "bar"—it means content that is set apart from a post or list of posts. In WordPress it's the widget holder.

The get_sidebar() template tag should replace the entire <aside></aside> right-hand sidebar on the home page and all of our other template pages. The get_sidebar() function works just like the get_header() and get_footer() functions. It locates sidebar.php in your theme files and inserts it in place of the function.

Try to remember that sidebar.php doesn't have to represent a sidebar, <aside>, or any other specific section of your site. Unfortunately, the term sidebar is no longer semantically correct and you should feel free to use the sidebar.php file anywhere in your theme.

We're actually going to need multiple sidebars: one for the right side of our template pages, and another for the area above the footer. The sidebar is traditionally used to house dynamic sidebars or widgets. We can actually do anything we want with them and, in this case, we're going to mix some static content with dynamic sidebar calls to generate this section of the site.

We'll learn exactly how to do all of this in the next chapter.

get_footer()

I hope you saw it coming: The last thing we need to do is insert the get_footer() function in the bottom of the index.php template file. Once again I've already broken up the template pages, so all you have to do is call the necessary functions. Once you're developing themes on your own, you'll have to find the right place to break the markup for the header, footer, and sidebars. Just try to remember to remove as much duplicate content as possible.

```
<?php get_footer(); ?>
```

Insert the above function as the absolute last thing in index.php.

What's Next

In the next chapter, we'll get our hands dirty with dynamic sidebars. This is going to be a fun chapter covering the use of widgets and how to display them correctly throughout our theme.

Dear WordPress Newcomer,

Monster Meltdown is an online marketplace that sells monster-sized design collections that web designers can use for inspiration in their projects. One of my first challenges when I conceived of the site was finding a membership system that would let me control access to content.

My first instinct was to consider the typical e-commerce systems, but they're not set up to connect with user management, at least not in a complex way. Furthermore, while traditional e-commerce can sell digital content, it is by no means a practical platform for publishing large amounts of content online.

On the flip side, systems that are set up to handle user membership and management are typically geared toward social communities. They make it hard to lock down content to controlled groups. And they have almost no connection to any kind of e-commerce or sales tool.

Fortunately, I found two solid WordPress plugins that became the foundation of the entire site:

- A user management plugin, which allows for user registration and gives me granular control over who can access what content. It lets me easily set up a group for each book so I can assign users to the books they have purchased.

- An e-commerce plugin specifically designed to connect to the user management plugin. This plugin lets me sell access to individual groups, thereby selling access to specific books.

You can find these on tipsandtricks-hq.com. They're commercial plugins, so they're not free, but they're priceless if you need this type of functionality. Check out their e-store and e-member plugins.

At the end of the day, WordPress provided a solid basis for my site and it lets me leverage numerous tools that every developer relies on. My only alternative would have been to custom-build something, which would have been far more time consuming and would essentially have made this project impossible. Instead, I can easily publish my content, sell access to it, and worry about marketing and promotion instead of fixing bugs and programming site logic.

Patrick McNeil
pmcneil.com| @designmeltdown

Dynamic Sidebars and Widgets

Sidebars are probably my favorite feature to build into a WordPress theme. They provide the highest level of customization to the user admin, enabling him to easily add new widgets, rearrange elements, and more. They empower him to make significant changes to the layout of the theme with inherent WordPress functionality.

What you're about to learn

- What sidebars and widgets are

- How to register sidebars

- How to add widgets

- How to create sidebar template files

- How to display dynamic sidebars

Sidebars and Widgets Defined

Sidebars and widgets are among the areas where WordPress needs to mature a bit. When theming for WordPress began, we utilized a very typical blogging design structure: the two-column layout. We'd put content on the left and a sidebar on the right. At that point, the term sidebar was very descriptive of its use. Today developers use sidebars and widgets in a variety of ways. Sidebars are placed throughout themes from headers to footers and every-where in between.

In early 2012, I wrote an article calling for two major changes in the way sidebars are defined. First, we need to give sidebars a new name so we can refer to them intelligently and correctly. Second, we need to stop making them theme dependent.

Currently, it's the web developer who defines (or registers) sidebars. When a sidebar is reg-istered, the developer gives it a name and places widgets into it. Since the developer is in charge of naming and there's no standard naming convention, the user admin risks losing all his widgets when he changes themes.

The solution I described in the article was to create widget locations that are a lot like menus. We'd allow the user admin to define widget holders and fill them with widgets. Then the developer would assign widget locations, which user admins could select to house their widget holders. For a more in-depth look at this recommendation, go to **http://wdgwp/sidebars-defined.**

For now, think of sidebars as widget holders. When a sidebar is registered, a widget holder appears in Appearance → Widgets. You can then drag your widgets into these holders. In the theme, you can call a WordPress function to display the sidebar by name. You'll be in charge of defining the HTML markup structure for the sidebar and the widgets. This gives you more control over how and where these sidebars are defined.

There's also a template page called sidebar.php that can house any amount of content but is meant to hold the output of the get_sidebar() function. You can define multiple sidebar tem-plate pages and call them as necessary.

Widgets are essentially WordPress plugins designed to create simple solutions for display-ing dynamic content. Typical widgets include recent posts, recent comments, links, menus, and search boxes, among others. You can write your own plugins to create your own wid-gets. Remember that "widgets" is a term used throughout the Web and is not specific to WordPress. Clients and user admins will often request a Facebook widget on their site. You have to remember the difference between the two and recognize that you may in fact use a WordPress widget for a Facebook widget.

The text and HTML widget in WordPress is one of the more powerful in the list because it lets you enter anything you want. It's easy to drop in a Facebook "Like" box, Twitter feed, or Flickr photo gallery.

Registering a Sidebar

Let's jump back into our functions.php file for this one. Registering a sidebar is easy and consistent with everything we've already learned. The register_sidebar() function accepts the following parameters:

```
$args = array(
    'name'          => '', //Sidebar Display Name
    'id'            => '', //sidebar-slug
    'description'   => '', //description (usually of location or function)
    'before_widget' => '', //HTML markup before the widget
    'after_widget'  => '', //HTML markup after the widget
    'before_title'  => '', //HTML markup before the widget title
    'after_title'   => '', //HTML markup after the widget title
);
```

Once you define the values of the above parameters, you need only pass them to the function like this:

```
register_sidebar( $args );
```

You can repeat the function above for as many sidebars as you need. However, the register_sidebars() (notice the pluralization) function lets us register several sidebars in one move. Registering multiple sidebars with a single function requires many of the parameters to be exactly the same, and this won't work for our theme. Instead, we'll repeat the register_sidebar(), passing different parameters as needed.

> **BEST PRACTICE**
>
> Registering a single sidebar or multiple sidebars is done in the functions.php file. It's important to plan the use of dynamic sidebars ahead of time so you can effectively code them into the theme. For more information on registering sidebars, check out the codex at http://wdgwp.com/register_sidebar and http://wdgwp.com/register_sidebars.

In Chapter 5, "Our First WordPress Website," we outlined the location of five different sidebars:

- The advertisements in the header

- The sidebar on the right-hand side of the theme

- The area above the footer

- The footer text on the left

- The footer text on the right

This may seem like a lot of widgets for one theme, but the goal is to limit the number of elements that are hard coded or that require the user admin to know HTML. If you're building a theme for yourself, your client, or your company, you'll likely feel more comfortable maintaining more HTML elements.

Header Sidebar

The header sidebar is an easy way for the user admin to add advertisements to the header. Since this is a sidebar, the user admin will be able to add any widget to the header and will need to make sure he doesn't break the theme. To create the first sidebar, insert the following code at the bottom of the functions.php file:

```php
$j2theme_header_sidebar = array(
   'name'            => 'Header',
   'id'              => 'header',
   'description'     => 'Widgets placed here will display in the header to the
         right of the logo',
   'before_widget'  => '',
   'after_widget'   => '',
   'before_title'   => '<h2>',
   'after_title'    => '</h2>',
);
register_sidebar( $j2theme_header_sidebar );
```

Notice the use of the prefix on the array name that is specific to the theme. This is a best practice for developers. We're not adding values to the before and after widget parameters because we want to drop the widgets into a containing div with no additional code surrounding each widget or title.

Once you save this code, you'll see a new sidebar in the Appearance → Widget section of the WordPress admin (**Figure 9.1**).

FIGURE 9.1
Header sidebar created in the WordPress admin.

Aside Sidebar

When registering the aside sidebar, pay close attention to the before and after widget parameters. Comparing this to output HTML makes it clear how these widgets will be generated:

```
$j2theme_aside_sidebar = array(
    'name'          => 'Aside',
    'id'            => 'aside',
    'description'   => 'Widgets placed here will go in the Right hand sidebar',
    'before_widget' => '<div class="widget">',
    'after_widget'  => '</div><!-- class: widget -->',
    'before_title'  => '<h3 class="widgettitle">',
    'after_title'   => '</h3>',
);
register_sidebar( $j2theme_aside_sidebar );.
```

This code creates an aside sidebar in the admin directly below the header sidebar. The order in which the sidebars appear in the admin is dictated by the order in which they're registered in the functions.php (**Figure 9.2**).

FIGURE 9.2
Aside sidebar created in the WordPress admin.

The HTML output from adding a recent posts widget to the aside sidebar is seen below. Notice that the output HTML is exactly as we had it in the register_sidebar() parameters.

```html
<div class="widget">
  <h3 class="widgettitle">Recent Posts</h3>
  <ul>
    <li><a href="http://localhost/j2-theme/hello-world" title="Hello
        World">Hello World</a></li>
    <li><a href="http://localhost/j2-theme/hello-world-again" title="Hello
        World Again">Hello World Again</a></li>
    <li><a href="http://localhost/j2-theme/hello-world-again-and-again"
        title="Hello World, Again and Again">Hello World, Again and Again
        </a></li>
    <li><a href="http://localhost/j2-theme/goodbye-world" title="Goodbye
        World">Goodbye World</a></li>
  </ul>
</div><!-- class: widget -->
```

It's important that the HTML is exactly as we created it in the template file, because we rely on the structure, class, and ID naming conventions to make sure the CSS correctly styles the content.

The next three widgets are very similar to the above two, but with changes in the parameter values.

Upper Footer Sidebar

The upper footer sidebar is shown in **Figure 9.3**.

```php
$j2theme_upperfooter_sidebar = array(
  'name'          => 'Upper Footer',
  'id'            => 'upper-footer',
  'description'   => 'Widgets placed here will go in the upper footer area ',
  'before_widget' => '<div class="widget">',
  'after_widget'  => '</div><!-- class: widget -->',
  'before_title'  => '<h3 class="widgettitle">',
  'after_title'   => '</h3>',
);
register_sidebar( $j2theme_upperfooter_sidebar );
```

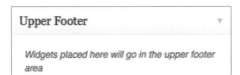

FIGURE 9.3
Upper footer sidebar created in the
WordPress admin.

Left Footer Sidebar

The left footer sidebar is shown in **Figure 9.4**.

```
$j2theme_footer_lt_sidebar = array(
    'name'          => 'Left Footer',
    'id'            => 'left-footer',
    'description'   => 'Widgets placed here will go in the left column of the
            footer',
    'before_widget' => '',
    'after_widget'  => '',
    'before_title'  => '<h3 class="widgettitle">',
    'after_title'   => '</h3>',
);
register_sidebar( $j2theme_footer_lt_sidebar );
```

Left Footer

*Widgets placed here will go in the left column
of the footer*

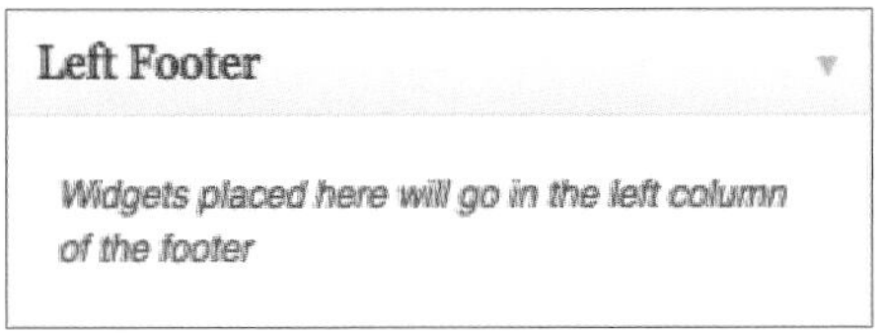

FIGURE 9.4
Left footer sidebar created in the
WordPress admin.

Right Footer Sidebar

The right footer sidebar is shown in **Figure 9.5**.

```
$j2theme_footer_rt_sidebar = array(
  'name'            => 'Right Footer',
  'id'              => 'right-footer',
  'description'     => 'Widgets placed here will go in the right column of the
        footer',
  'before_widget' => '',
  'after_widget'  => '',
  'before_title'  => '<h3 class="widgettitle">',
  'after_title'   => '</h3>',
);
register_sidebar( $j2theme_footer_rt_sidebar );
```

Right Footer

Widgets placed here will go in the right column of the footer

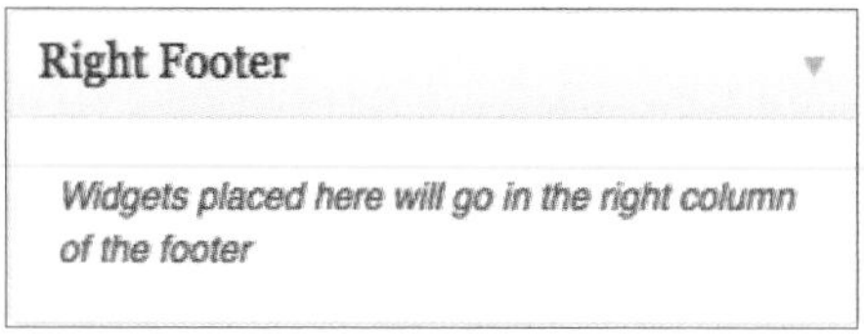

FIGURE 9.5
Right footer sidebar created in the WordPress admin.

Adding Widgets

Now that the sidebars are in place, we need to fill them with widgets. Feel free to use any widgets you want for testing purposes. Once you add the widgets to the sidebars, you can remove them, rearrange them, or save them simply by dragging them (**Figure 9.6**).

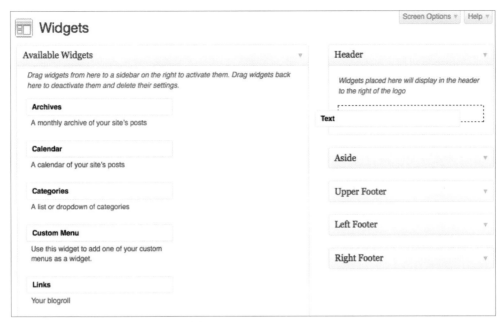

FIGURE 9.6 Adding widgets to the sidebars.

■■■ NOTE

As of WordPress 3.4, you'll be able to drag widgets into the Inactive Widgets area (**Figure 9.7**) to be reimplemented later. There's also an Inactive Sidebars section that will make it easier to restore a sidebar if your new theme no longer supports it. This is a great step in the right direction for better widget utilization.

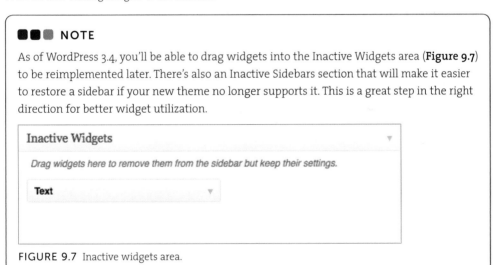

FIGURE 9.7 Inactive widgets area.

get_sidebar();

Having five sidebars to implement throughout the theme might get a bit confusing. To help alleviate that confusion, I've commented the template files pretty heavily. Look for the comments seen below to help you place the get_sidebar() functions throughout the template files:

```
<!-- Start get_sidebar() -->
<!-End get_sidebar() -->
```

Everything in between those comments, including the comments themselves, should be replaced with:

```
<?php get_sidebar(); ?>
```

The get_sidebar() function locates sidebar.php in the theme files and replaces the function with everything inside that file. Sidebar.php acts as the default sidebar and houses the aside sidebar. We'll also create sidebar files with specific names for each sidebar location.

Take a second to create the following files:

- sidebar-header.php

- sidebar-upper-footer.php

- sidebar-lt-footer.php

- sidebar-rt-footer.php

We'll call these files using the get_sidebar() function, but this time we'll pass a parameter that matches the file name (after "sidebar-" and without .php). Utilize the following code to call the respective sidebars in the correct locations in all of the template files:

```
<?php get_sidebar( 'header' ); ?> <!-- sidebar-header.php -->
<?php get_sidebar( 'upper-footer' ); ?> <!-- sidebar- upper-footer.php -->
<?php get_sidebar( 'lt-footer' ); ?> <!-- sidebar-lt-footer.php -->
<?php get_sidebar( 'rt-footer' ); ?> <!-- sidebar-rt-footer.php -->
```

Now that we're calling the sidebar template files correctly, we need to actually pull the dynamic sidebars into these files.

dynamic_sidebar()

In true WordPress development fashion, the call to pull in the dynamic sidebars is as easy as calling the dynamic_sidebar() function and passing it a parameter. The parameter we're passing is the name of the sidebar that we chose when we registered it. Don't pass the slug; use the full name of the sidebar:

```php
<?php dynamic_sidebar( 'Header' ) ; ?> <!-- Place into sidebar-header.php -->
<?php dynamic_sidebar( 'Aside' ); ?> <!-- Place into sidebar.php -->
<?php dynamic_sidebar( 'Upper Footer' ); ?> <!-- Place into sidebar-upper-
        footer.php -->
<?php dynamic_sidebar( 'Left Footer' ); ?> <!-- sidebar-lt-footer.php -->
<?php dynamic_sidebar( 'Right Footer' ); ?> <!-- sidebar-rt-footer.php -->
```

Once you've placed the dynamic_sidebar() functions into the correct sidebars, you'll see the widgets appear throughout the WordPress website. You now have full control over the widget areas and these sidebars. Feel free to add, remove, or rearrange widgets at will.

What's Next?

Chapter 10, "Single," is all about the single.php template file, which is used for posts. We'll create a loop made just for a single post item, pull in metadata, and even display comments and a comment form.

Single

This chapter is aptly named "Single" because the template theme file used to display a single post is called single.php. The single.php template is used anytime a user is on a post page (or nonhierarchical custom post type). Typically, the difference between the single and page template that powers a single page is additional metadata (dates, author, comment number) and the Comments section.

What you're about to learn

- Additional Template Tags for pulling post data

- How to display author information

- How to enable commenting on a post

- How to display the comment form and styling the comments template

Post Page Layout

The post template page has a structure similar to the rest of the site (**Figure 10.1**). The header, footer, and sidebar are exactly the same as on the home page. The only area that's different is the content area on the left. This is why it's so important not to duplicate the code used to support the areas that are the same throughout the theme.

The content area starts with a featured image at the top. This file is used throughout the site, but here it's cropped at a different size. Later, we'll define the different sizes for all featured images.

Below the featured image is the title of the post, then the date and number of comments. This time the number of comments anchors to the Comments section below.

The content is pulled in with a single template tag, and that will display anything in the content editor, including text, images, videos, and more. Under the content are links to the categories and tags (taxonomy) this post is assigned to. The pagination for this section is different from the home page; this time it links only to the previous and next posts (based on date).

It's important to pull in the author information, especially if your site has many contributors. While authors are not always users and users are not necessarily authors, we'll power the Authors section with data from the user profiles. If you have a contributing author, it makes sense to create a user account for her. She won't need login credentials and you can always lower her role as well.

The Comments section has many parts, but WordPress has a prebuilt comments template that we'll be using. This makes it easy to generate all the HTML for this section, including the form. You'll have the option to edit the template or create your own if you so choose.

FIGURE 10.1
The Post template page.

The Loop

The Loop will remain identical to the one on the home page. The only difference is what goes inside it. Also, since we're not running iterations of posts, we don't have to worry about the actual duplicating of HTML structure. In this case, there will be only one post per loop.

Having a while here doesn't hurt, but it's not necessary because there's only one post:

```
<?php if ( have_posts() ) : while ( have_posts() ) : the_post(); ?>
  <!-- PLACE EVERYTHING FROM FEATURED IMAGE TO COMMMENTS -->
<?php endwhile; else: ?>
  <p><?php _e( 'The post you're looking for could not be found.' ); ?></p>
<?php endif; ?>
```

All the code that follows in this chapter will be placed in the loop above.

Article Header

The article header tag contains the featured image, title tag, and post metadata (**Figure 10.2**). Everything that follows will be placed in the <header> tag in the <article> tag.

FIGURE 10.2 Article header.

Featured Image

Displaying a specific featured image based on its size requires some code that we haven't written yet. We'll look at how to do this in a later chapter, and at that time we'll come back and replace this. For now, just so we know the theme is working, replace the featured <img> tag at the top of the template with:

```php
<?php the_post_thumbnail(); ?>
```

This is exactly how we did it in The Loop on the home page.

Title

The title of the post is displayed with the the_title() template tag. It doesn't need an <a> tag around it because, unlike on the home page, we're not linking the title to the post. Inside the <h1> tags, replace the content with:

```php
<?php the_title(); ?>
```

This outputs the following HTML:

```html
<h1>Hello World</h1>
```

Post Metadata

For the post date and number of comments, grab the code straight from the index.php template. Nothing is changing here except that we're linking to the comments below. I added an <a> tag around the comments number anchoring to the #comments div below:

```php
<p>Posted <time datetime="<?php the_time('Y-m-d'); ?>" pubdate="pubdate">
    <?php the_time('M n'); ?></time> &#149; <a href="#comments"><?php
    comments_number( '0 comments', 'only 1 comment', '% comments' ); ?>
    </a></p>
```

The Template Tags the_time() and comments_number() are discussed in great detail in Chapter 8, "Home Page."

Content

On the home page we didn't actually pull in any content from the content editor (**Figure 10.3**). Each post had a title, date, comment count, and featured image. In later chapters we'll take a closer look at conditionals like if statements and alternatives to the featured image on the home page. For example, if there's no featured image on a post, you can either remove it from the list on the home page or pull in the excerpt.

The text above is just large intro text. Smaller paragraph text will be entered here. Lorem ipsum dolor sit amet, consectetur adipiscing elit. Fusce scelerisque libero non mauris ultrices vehicula. Aliquam eleifend vehicula velit, et pharetra tellus ornare eu. In volutpat, justo interdum viverra euismod, purus nulla dapibus mauris, sed placerat est quam non tortor. Phasellus semper rutrum lacus. Nam feugiat mollis dapibus. Sed et elit rutrum metus mollis pharetra. Nulla ante sem, suscipit ullamcorper auctor et, eleifend at lectus. Nunc at augue dui. In volutpat, justo interdum viverra euismod, purus nulla dapibus mauris, sed placerat est quam non tortor. Phasellus semper rutrum lacus. Nam feugiat mollis dapibus. Sed et elit rutrum metus mollis pharetra. The text above is just large intro text. Smaller paragraph text will be entered here. Lorem ipsum dolor sit amet, consectetur adipiscing elit. Fusce scelerisque libero non mauris ultrices vehicula. Aliquam eleifend vehicula velit, et pharetra tellus ornare eu. In volutpat, justo interdum viverra euismod, purus nulla dapibus mauris, sed placerat est quam non tortor. Phasellus semper rutrum lacus. Nam feugiat mollis dapibus. Sed et elit rutrum metus mollis pharetra. Nulla ante sem, suscipit ullamcorper auctor et, eleifend at lectus. Nunc at augue dui. In volutpat, justo interdum viverra euismod, purus nulla dapibus mauris, sed placerat est quam non tortor. Phasellus semper rutrum lacus. Nam feugiat mollis dapibus. Sed et elit rutrum metus mollis pharetra. The text above is just large intro text. Smaller paragraph text will be entered here. Lorem ipsum dolor sit amet, consectetur adipiscing elit. Fusce scelerisque libero non mauris ultrices vehicula. Aliquam

FIGURE 10.3 The content.

The excerpt is a shortened version of the content. You can either have the the_excerpt() Template Tag pull content that you define in the excerpt editor on the post, or pull the first bit of content in the content editor with images and special formatting stripped.

Since we're on the Post page it only makes sense to show the full content. Some themes use the excerpt in the single.php template page to show what's coming up in the next post:

```
<?php the_content(); ?>
```

This Template Tag or WordPress call displays all the content in the content editor. This includes, but is not limited to, text, HTML, images, graphics, videos, and even shortcodes (which we'll discuss in later chapters).

Unless you've specifically stated otherwise, any content that's not wrapped in HTML already will be wrapped in <p> tags. You can turn this off by disabling the wpautop filter in the functions.php file. However, most of the time the auto-wrapping comes in handy and is the default functionality in most themes.

Since we don't have to worry about the HTML markup for each element in the content editor, all we do is place the the_content() function in the content div like so:

```
<div class="content">
  <?php the_content(); ?>
</div><!-- content -->
```

You can read more about the_content at http://wdgwp.com/the_content and about the_excerpt at http://wdgwp.com/the_excerpt.

Article Footer

The footer has several components, including the taxonomy, author information, and pagination (Figure 10.4).

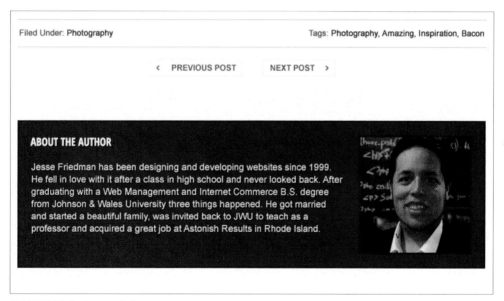

FIGURE 10.4 The article footer.

Taxonomy

It's important to give users a way to continue reading through your site. Increasing time on site leads to better conversion, commenting, and sharing—and more return visits.

> **BEST PRACTICE**
>
> One way to keep users clicking is to provide ways to read more related posts. One of my favorite plugins, YARPP (Yet Another Related Posts Plugin), displays a list of posts related to the one you're reading. A simple solution that requires no plugins and is always a best practice is listing the categories and tags a post is assigned to.

A nicely displayed list of categories and tags may prompt a visitor to click through to another page. Displaying the categories and tags is, not surprisingly, easy to do:

```
<div class="tax">
  <div class="alignleft">
    <p>Filed under: <!-- category list --></p>
  </div>
  <div class="alignright txtrt">
    <p><!-- tags list --></p>
  </div>
</div><!-- tax -->
```

The taxonomy <div> is structured pretty simply. All we have to do is call replace the commented-out code with the categories and tags calls. Replace <!-- category list --> with:

```
<?php the_category( ', ' ); ?>
```

The the_category() function accepts a few parameters. Here we're going to pass only one, the separator. Since the the_category() function returns a list of category titles wrapped in <a> tags linking to the respective archive pages, we need to define what we want between each item on the list. In our case, we'll have a comma-separated list so we'll pass ", ". Notice the space after the comma: Without this there will be no space between each category. For more info on the_category(), go to **http://wdgwp.com/the_category**.

Next replace <!-- tags list --> with the_tags() function. This function accepts similar parameters to its cousin the_category(), but since the defaults are perfect for our use we don't have to override them by passing any parameters. The one thing we want to avoid is having the <div> containing the tags ever be empty:

```php
<?php if( get_the_tags() ) { ?>
    <div class="alignright txtrt">
      <p><?php the_tags(); ?></p>
    </div>
<?php } ?>
```

In this case we'll wrap the div in an if statement. We'll look at conditionals and if statements in greater detail later, but for now just know that we're asking if the get_the_tags() function is returning a value. Many WordPress functions that start with get_ return a value you can use to test against or put into a variable. Here, removing the get_ calls a different but similar function that automatically outputs its values as HTML. You can read more about this at http://wdgwp.com/the_tags.

When all is said and done, the taxonomy div should be coded like this:

```php
<div class="tax">
  <div class="alignleft">
    <p>Filed under: <?php the_category( ', ' ); ?></p>
  </div>
  <?php if( get_the_tags() ) { ?>
    <div class="alignright txtrt">
      <p><?php the_tags(); ?></p>
    </div>
  <?php } ?>
</div><!-- tax -->
```

You may be wondering why we didn't put an if statement around the category call. Unlike a tag, a post must be assigned to at least one category. If you don't choose a category, then the post will be auto-assigned to the default category. Tags are optional and we don't want empty divs in our finished website, so we'll make sure that the post has tags before we output the HTML.

Author

The author div has the author's name at the top, linking to the respective archive page (a list of all the author's posts), her Gravatar, description, and URL:

```
<div class="author">
  <h3>Written by: <!-- author name and archives link --></h3>
  <!-- Gravatar -->
  <p><!-- description --></p>
  <a href="<!-- author url -->" title="<!-- author's first name -->'s
      Website" target="_blank"><!-- author url --></a>
</div><!-- author -->
```

I've laid out the author div HTML structure above. We have a few different elements to display. The author name and archives link can actually be called with a single function. Replace <!-- author name and archives link --> with:

```
<?php the_author_posts_link(); ?>
```

Since every post needs an author and all authors have archive links, there's no need to test for the existence of this content as we did with tags. This function automatically generates an <a> tag with a link to the archive and displays the author's "display name." See http://wdgwp.com/author_link.

The author's avatar will actually be a Gravatar. Gravatar is short for "globally recognized avatar." You can get a Gravatar by signing up at http://wdgwp.com/Gravatar. Once you have a Gravatar, anyone who has your e-mail address can request it to be displayed. In this case, the e-mail address associated with the user profile dictates whether or not she gets an image displayed next to her name. WordPress has a rather nice function used to retrieve the Gravatar of the user. Replace <!-- Gravatar --> with:

```
<?php echo get_avatar( get_the_author_meta( 'email' ), '50', 'Mystery Man',
    'Avatar of ' . get_the_author_meta( 'first_name' ) . '
    ' . get_the_author_meta( 'last_name' ) ); ?>
```

This single line of code performs several functions at once. First, it echoes the result of the get_avatar() function, which will return an <img> tag complete with a URL to the avatar. If the author doesn't have a Gravatar set up, the image will default to the "Mystery Man" or other default setting.

The parameters are set by functions and specific values alike, as outlined below:

1. The ID or e-mail used to retrieve the avatar: get_the_author_meta('email')

2. Size of the avatar: 50

3. Default avatar to use if Gravatar is missing: Mystery Man

4. Alt text for the <img> tag: 'Avatar of ' . get_the_author_meta('first_name') . ' '
   . get_the_author_meta('last_name') (adding values to functions)

All these functions output the following HTML:

```
<img alt='Avatar of Jesse Friedman' src='http://0.gravatar.com/avatar/09
    34fa64cc323b6a2e10dc37fc33fa64?s=50&amamp;d=Mystery+Man&amp;r=G'
    class='avatar avatar-50 photo' height='50' width='50' />
```

I know that was a lot to take in, but in the end all we're doing is making calls to output HTML. The rest of the Authors section will be far less complex, I promise.

The author's description, usually referred to as a bio, is defined in the user profile. Only text will be accepted in this field, so we'll wrap it in a <p> tag. Replace <!-- description --> with:

```
<?php if( get_the_author_meta( 'description' ) ) { ?>
<p><?php the_author_meta( 'description' ); ?></p>
<?php } ?>
```

Once again we have to test for the existence of the description. We don't want to force the author to put in a bio; that's bad form. We just don't want to output empty <p> tags if there's no bio.

The the_author_meta() function outputs any number of details about the author of the current post. You can pass it several parameters; in this case, we're requesting the description. Above, we used the get_the_author_meta() function to return the e-mail and first and last names of the author. For more info on these functions go to http://wdgwp.com/the_author_meta and http://wdgwp.com/get_the_author_meta.

Next we want to display the author's URL. If the author is a contributor, it's nice to link to the author's site as a thank you. If you operate the site and are the author, you can put your Twitter or Facebook URL in place. Since we didn't put the word "Website" between the <a></a> tags, anything placed in the author's website field on the user profile page will go nicely here.

Replace the following HTML:

```
<a href="<!-- author url -->" title="<!-- author's first name -->'s Website"
    target="_blank"><!-- author url --></a>
```

with:

```
<?php if( get_the_author_meta( 'user_url' ) ) { ?>
<a href="<?php the_author_meta( 'user_url' ); ?>" title="<?php
    the_author_meta( 'first_name' ); ?>'s Website" target="_blank">
    <?php the_author_meta( 'user_url' ); ?></a>
<?php } ?>
```

At this point the code above should make sense to you. If not, please reread the last few pages. It's important for you to be able to interpret code as it's written. Anything that doesn't make sense can be referenced in earlier examples of code or in the WordPress Codex.

The entire author div should now look like this:

```
<div class="author">
  <h3>Written by: <?php the_author_posts_link(); ?></h3>
  <?php echo get_avatar( get_the_author_meta( 'email' ), '50', 'Mystery Man',
      'Avatar of ' . get_the_author_meta( 'first_name' ) . '
      ' . get_the_author_meta( 'last_name' ) ); ?>
  <?php if( get_the_author_meta( 'description' ) ) { ?>
    <p><?php the_author_meta( 'description' ); ?> </p>
  <?php } ?>
  <?php if( get_the_author_meta( 'user_url' ) ) { ?>
    <a href="<?php the_author_meta( 'user_url' ); ?>" title="<?php
        the_author_meta( 'first_name' ); ?>'s Website" target="_blank">
        <?php the_author_meta( 'user_url' ); ?></a>
  <?php } ?>
</div><!-- author -->
```

The HTML below is an example of what will be output, assuming I'm the author of the post:

```html
<div class="author">
  <h3>Written by: <a href="http://localhost/j2-theme/author/jfriedman/"
      title="Posts by Jesse Friedman" rel="author">Jesse Friedman</a></h3>
  <img alt='Avatar of Jesse Friedman' src='http://0.gravatar.com/avatar/
      0934fa64cc323b6a2e10dc37fc33fa64?s=50&amp;d=Mystery+Man&amp;r=G'
      class='avatar avatar-50 photo' height='50' width='50' />
<p>I'm a professor, author, speaker and developer. I love WordPress,
    especially teaching it. </p>
  <a href="http://jesserfriedman.com" title="Jesse's Website"
      target="_blank">http://jesserfriedman.com</a>
</div><!-- author -->
```

Pagination

To help make it easy to continue browsing our site, we want to provide simple buttons leading to the previous and next posts. Unlike the pagination on the home page, where we link to archive pages, here we'll be linking to specific posts. The Previous and Next buttons are easy to generate with WordPress functions.

Directly below the closing author </div> is the <nav> tag. In there is an unordered list. We'll replace the content in the <li> tags with the following functions:

```php
previous_post_link();
next_post_link();
```

These functions output an <a> tag with a link to the corresponding post and, by default, its title. For this theme we'll replace the title of the post and have "< Previous Post" and "Next Post >" as the text on the buttons. To do this, we need to pass two parameters to the functions:

```php
<ul>
  <?php previous_post_link( '<li>%link</li>', '&lt; Previous Post' ); ?>
  <?php next_post_link( '<li>%link</li>', 'Next Post &gt;' ); ?>
</ul>
```

The first parameter dictates the treatment of the link. We're wrapping the %link with <li></li> tags because if there is no previous or next link, we don't want empty HTML tags. You won't have a previous or next link if you're viewing the first or last posts in the blog, since there's nothing to continue to. The second parameter is what actually goes in between the <a></a> tags. I've escaped the "<" and ">," which is why you see "<" and ">". For more information on these Template Tags go to http://wdgwp.com/previous_post_link and http://wdgwp.com/next_post_link.

The previous code outputs the following HTML:

```
<ul>
  <li><a href="http://localhost/j2-theme/hello-world/" rel="prev">&lt;
      Previous Post</a></li>
  <li><a href="http://localhost/j2-theme/hello-world-again-and-again/"
      rel="next">Next Post &gt;</a></li>
</ul>
```

Comments

The Comments section is a pretty heavy area (**Figure 10.5**). Coding every aspect of it can be difficult and time-consuming. A specific comment has the author's avatar, name, website URL, comment, and reply link. Threaded comments require special thought, and there's the Comments form itself to build. You have to perform special actions for logged-in versus other users, compare that against approved and unapproved comments, and more.

Luckily for us WordPress has a built-in comments template that generates all of this for us. The comments template is built into the WordPress core. If you want to create your own template you can pass the location of that template as a parameter in the comments_template() function, which we're about to use. Either way, you need a comments.php file in your theme (as of WordPress 3.0). You can locate the default comments.php file wp-includes → theme-compat. If it isn't there already, copy the comments.php into your theme folder:

```
<?php comments_template(); ?>
```

Drop the above function into the Comments section of the post template. We're not going to pass any parameters to this function, but if you like you can pull your own comments template like this:

```
<?php comments_template( '/my-comments-template.php' ); ?>
```

The my-comments-template.php file would be placed in the theme directory with the rest of your files. For more information on the comments_template() function and creating your own comments template go to http://wdgwp.com/comments_template.

FIGURE 10.5
Comments.

In this theme only posts can be commented on. The comments capability and template can be implemented into a page template if you so choose. In addition, any of the Template Tags we've used for the post can be placed on a page template (with the exception of categories and tags, as we can't assign pages to those taxonomies). You can create your own comments template to define exactly how the layout and functions work in your theme.

Calling the comments_template() displays all of the approved comments on the current post and includes the Comments form at the bottom, which has the following fields:

- Name

- Mail

- Website

- Comment

WordPress validates the form for you and submits the data. Once the comment is submitted, depending on the site settings, it may display immediately. Based on the default comments template, every comment can be "replied" to, creating a thread of comments. The depth of that thread will be defined by the comments settings in the admin.

The comments template outputs the following HTML on an example post with three comments, one of which is a reply. I've removed some irrelevant content to save space:

```
<h3 id="comments">3 Responses to &#8220;Hello world!&#8221;</h3>


<ol class="commentlist">
  <li class="comment even thread-even depth-1 parent" id="comment-1">
    <div id="div-comment-1" class="comment-body">
      <div class="comment-author vcard">
        <img alt='' src='http://0.gravatar.com/avatar/ad516503a11cd5ca435
        acc9bb6523536?s=32' class='avatar avatar-32 photo avatar-default'
        height='32' width='32' />
        <cite class="fn"><a href='http://wordpress.org/' rel='external
        nofollow' class='url'>Mr WordPress</a></cite>
        <span class="says">says:</span>
      </div>
      <div class="comment-meta commentmetadata">
        <a href="http://localhost/j2-theme/hello-world/#comment-1">May 4,
        2012 at 6:27 pm</a>
      </div>
      <p>Hi, this is a comment.<br />To delete a comment, just log in and
        view the post&#039;s comments. There you will have the option to edit
        or delete them.</p>
      <div class="reply">
        <a class='comment-reply-link' href='/j2-theme/hello-
        world/?replytocom=1#respond' onclick='return addComment.
        moveForm("div-comment-1", "1", "respond", "1")'>Reply</a>
```

continues on next page

```
        </div>
      </div>
      <ul class='children'>
        <li class="comment odd alt depth-2" id="comment-7">
          <div id="div-comment-7" class="comment-body">
            <div class="comment-author vcard">
              <img alt='' src='http://1.gravatar.com/avatar/bb9b1e9ed6ac9b3d73e
35aa2a1eca8b7?s=32&amp;d=http%3A%2F%2F1.gravatar.com%2Favatar%2Fad516
503a11cd5ca435acc9bb6523536%3Fs%3D32&amp;r=G' class='avatar avatar-32
photo' height='32' width='32' />
              <cite class="fn"><a href='http://jesserfriedman.com' rel='external
nofollow' class='url'>Jesse Friedman</a></cite>
              <span class="says">says:</span>
            </div>
            <div class="comment-meta commentmetadata">
              <a href="http://localhost/j2-theme/hello-world/#comment-7">May
20, 2012 at 3:36 am</a>
            </div>
            <p>That&#8217;s a great point. Thanks for sharing.</p>
            <div class="reply">
              <a class='comment-reply-link' href='/j2-theme/hello-
world/?replytocom=7#respond' onclick='return addComment.
moveForm("div-comment-7", "7", "respond", "1")'>Reply</a>
            </div>
          </div>
        </li>
      </ul>
    </li>
    <li class="comment even thread-odd thread-alt depth-1" id="comment-8">
      <div id="div-comment-8" class="comment-body">
        <div class="comment-author vcard">
          <img alt='' src='http://0.gravatar.com/avatar/6a6c19fea4a3676970167c
e51f39e6ee?s=32&amp;d=http%3A%2F%2F0.gravatar.com%2Favatar%2Fad51650
3a11cd5ca435acc9bb6523536%3Fs%3D32&amp;r=G' class='avatar avatar-32
photo' height='32' width='32' />

          <cite class="fn"><a href='http://doe.com' rel='external nofollow'
class='url'>John Doe</a></cite>
```

continues on next page

```
        <span class="says">says:</span>
      </div>
      <div class="comment-meta commentmetadata">
        <a href="http://localhost/j2-theme/hello-world/#comment-8">May 20,
        2012 at 3:37 am</a>
      </div>
      <p>I really agree with this post, it&#8217;s something I do everyday.</p>
      <div class="reply">
        <a class='comment-reply-link' href='/j2-theme/hello-world/
        ?replytocom=8#respond' onclick='return addComment.moveForm("div-
        comment-8", "8", "respond", "1")'>Reply</a>
      </div>
    </div>
  </li>
</ol>
<div id="respond">
  <h3>Leave a Reply</h3>
  <div id="cancel-comment-reply">
    <form action="http://localhost/j2-theme/wp-comments-post.php"
        method="post" id="commentform">
      <p><input type="text" name="author" id="author" value="John
        Doe" size="22" tabindex="1" aria-required='true' /><label
        for="author"><small>Name (required)</small></label></p>
      <p><input type="text" name="email" id="email" value="john@doe.com"
        size="22" tabindex="2" aria-required='true' /><label for="email">
        <small>Mail (will not be published) (required)</small></label></p>

      <p><input type="text" name="url" id="url" value="http://doe.com" size="22"
        tabindex="3" /><label for="url"><small>Website</small></label></p>

      <p><textarea name="comment" id="comment" cols="58" rows="10"
        tabindex="4"></textarea></p>

      <p><input name="submit" type="submit" id="submit" tabindex="5"
        value="Submit Comment" /><input type='hidden' name='comment_post_ID'
        value='1' id='comment_post_ID' /><input type='hidden'
        name='comment_parent' id='comment_parent' value='0' /></p>

    </form>
  </div>
</div>
```

I know that was a lot of HTML to look through, but as you can see, many elements go into making the Comments section. Note that the comments are basically an ordered list and that threaded comments are list items inside list items. It's very similar to a basic drop-down nav structure.

It may seem intimidating to create your own comments template, especially if you only need to make a small change. If, for example, your theme doesn't have the commenter's avatar displayed, it would make sense to customize the comments template and remove those avatars. However, this may be a bit advanced for you at the moment and, if that's the case, you can use CSS to hide or alter elements. This isn't exactly a best practice because we're loading the avatars and hiding them, but it's one solution to get you where you need to be.

What's Next

Adding the Comments section to the post template was the last piece of the puzzle. In the next chapter, we'll build the page template and talk about custom page templates that let the user admin decide how her page content will be displayed.

Dear New Kid on the WordPress Block,

I remember the first time I was asked to do anything with WordPress was for a design house that often hired me to code sites from PSD files to PHP or SHTML. The client asked me to troubleshoot an issue they were having, and since WordPress was (and still is) PHP-based, I figured it would be no problem. I still remember my reaction when I opened a template file to look at the code: my brain immediately fired off alarm warnings, my brow creased, and I'm pretty sure I uttered an expletive.

I laugh now recalling that moment, because I really knew nothing. The request was simply to fix a heading, but it took me close to two days to sort it out. I was so intrigued by what I came across in those two days that I simply had to learn more.

These days, WordPress really is a lot easier, especially if you have a basic knowledge of writing PHP or HTML. My best advice to new WordPress inductees is simply this: set yourself up with a localhost system (or a directory on your server), install WordPress on it, and play with it. As in life, make mistakes! Experience is gained through those mistakes, as well as your successes.

WordPress is a joy, and it begs to be played with. Try to break it, and when you do, don't freak out—it's easy to fix! Come up with some really whacked-out ideas and try to implement them. Study the codex, and books like this one. Consult with other people in the WordPress community. Playing with WordPress—testing its limits and seeing what you can make it do—will give you great experience that you can pass on to your clients.

And as with anything in our industry, never think you know it all—always be willing to learn the newest thing. Join the WordPress lists to get access to the newest versions before they're even released for beta testing to the public. You'll never regret it, and you get to play with the cool toys before anyone else does!

Shelly Cole
brassblogs.com | @brassblogs

Page

You'll notice that the word "page" is used repetitively throughout this chapter. We're going to look at how to create the base page template, page.php, as well as some additional custom page templates. Page templates are used to display page content and, if custom page templates are defined, the user admin will have more control over the design of his pages.

What you're about to learn

- Page template best practices

- How to display page content

- How to create custom page templates

- How the user admin defines which template to use in the admin

Page Page Layout

A quick glance at **Figure 11.1** shows just how similar the Page page template is to the single page template and the rest of the site. We still have the featured image at the top of the page, the title, and the main content. However, we don't have the date, comments count, taxonomy, pagination, or author information. In fact, the comments functionality doesn't exist on the page templates at all. If you'd like to allow commenting on your pages, you can call the comments_template() function as we discussed in Chapter 10, "Single."

We're adding two new elements to the page template. The first is breadcrumb navigation that shows the path back to the home page from the current location. The second is a tagline, which is actually powered by the excerpt.

By now you should have a pretty good idea of how we're going to convert the static HTML to dynamic WordPress calls. Later in the chapter we'll discuss creating additional custom page templates and empowering the user admin to choose between them.

Everything will be called in the same loop that we used in the single.php template.

The Loop

We're not requiring anything new or custom for our loop, so at this point it will remain the same:

```php
<?php if ( have_posts() ) : while ( have_posts() ) : the_post(); ?>
  <! -- PLACE EVERYTHING FROM FEATURED IMAGE TO CONTENT -->
<?php endwhile; else: ?>
  <p><?php _e( 'The page you're looking for could not be found.' ); ?></p>
<?php endif; ?>
```

FIGURE 11.1
The Page page template.

Page Header

The page header contains the featured image, breadcrumb navigation, page title, and tagline (Figure 11.2). The featured image and title should be pretty straightforward for you by now. The breadcrumb navigation will require a specially made function and the tagline will require us to turn on the excerpt functionality for pages.

FIGURE 11.2
The Page page template header.

Featured Image

As we did in Chapter 10, "Single," we'll replace the basic the_post_thumbnail() call later when we learn more about featured images. For now, replace the featured image HTML with:

```php
<?php the_post_thumbnail(); ?>
```

Breadcrumb Navigation

Breadcrumb navigation is especially helpful for users who arrive at your site on an interior page. Google serves up interior pages on Search Engine Results Pages (SERPs) now more than ever. Breadcrumb navigation provides a trail back to the home page that helps the visitor understand where he is in the site and shows him more helpful page links that he might have otherwise missed.

Typically we start with the home page, then list pages, child pages, grandchildren, and so on. So if we're on my bio page, which is under my company profile About Us page, the breadcrumb navigation would display:

Home → About Us → Jesse Friedman

To do this we need to make sure that our pages are correctly organized in the admin, using page hierarchy. To create a child page, you'll need to choose a parent page under the Page Attributes section on the Edit Page page, as seen in **Figure 11.3**.

FIGURE 11.3
Adding a page parent.

When you add a parent page you can also choose the page order. This will come in handy when you work with sibling pages or use a page list to create navigation.

Once you add child pages you can see the page hierarchy coming into effect by going to the All Pages page in the admin (**Figure 11.4**).

	Title	Author	💬	Date
☐	**About Us**	Jesse Friedman	💬	2 mins ago Published
☐	**— Jeff Golenski**	Jesse Friedman	💬	1 min ago Published
☐	**— Jesse Friedman**	Jesse Friedman	💬	2 mins ago Published
☐	Title	Author	💬	Date

FIGURE 11.4 Page hierarchy.

The next part displays the current page title, its parent, their parents, and so on all the way back to the home page, and requires a decent amount of custom code. While it's extremely satisfying to develop your own solution to a problem like this, sometimes it's just better to not reinvent the wheel. The plugin appendix at the end of this book goes into detail about some of the better plugins out there; Breadcrumb NavXT is included in that list.

Installing Breadcrumb NavXT is really simple. Go to Plugins → Add New in the admin. Once there, type in "Breadcrumb NavXT" into the search box. This plugin has a high rating and has been downloaded over 500,000 times, plus it's highly recommended by many developers. (As stated before, it's important to do your plugin research prior to installing and activating.)

BEST PRACTICE

When developing themes for reuse it's never a good idea to rely on functions that will not be defined by your theme or in the WordPress core. In this case we're calling a function created by a plugin we installed. Don't assume that a user admin who installs your theme will install the Breadcrumb NavXT plugin.

Once you install and activate the plugin, you can navigate to its Settings page by going to Settings → Breadcrumb NavXT, as shown in **Figure 11.5**.

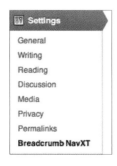

FIGURE 11.5
Breadcrumb NavXT Settings tab.

Once you configure the settings, the next step is to display the breadcrumb nav on the site. On the page.php template, locate the <nav></nav> tags in the <header> of the page content section and replace it with:

```
<nav class="breadcrumb">
    <p><?php if( function_exists( 'bcn_display' ) ) {
        bcn_display();
    } ?></p>
</nav><!-- breadcrumb -->
```

The bcn_display() function is defined by the plugin; this is not a WordPress core function or Template Tag. The function_exists() function returns "true" or "false" depending on whether the function bcn_display actually exists and is callable by the code. If you don't perform this check and call an undefined function, you'll receive a fatal error, and the site will not load for the user. This is especially important when you're calling something that's defined by an outside source like a plugin. The call above outputs HTML <a> tags with the page titles and separators defined in the settings:

```
<nav class="breadcrumb">
    <p><a title="Go to Home." href="http://localhost/j2-theme">Home</a>
        &raquo; <a title="Go to About Us." href="http://localhost/j2-theme/
        about-us/">About Us</a> &raquo; Jesse Friedman</p>
</nav><!-- breadcrumb -->
```

If you're interested in writing your own function to display the breadcrumb navigation go to http://wdgwp.com/breadcrumb, where you'll find some great articles and resources to walk you through the rest of the process.

Title

Replace the static title in the page template with the code below. It's important to try and write this out every time you implement it: This will help you better remember the specific function names, and help you get used to writing PHP.

```
<?php the_title(); ?>
```

Use the above code to replace the <h1> tags in the <header> of the page content area.

Tagline

Below the title is a section where you can display a tagline or page excerpt. There are several ways to accomplish this, the best being to define custom meta fields in the page, similar to the custom post type. This discussion is outside the scope of this book, however, so for now you can just turn on excerpt function for pages and use that for the tagline. This still makes sense because the content entered here would still semantically be an excerpt.

The first thing to do is turn on the excerpt function for pages. This isn't inherently built into WordPress, so we have to do it manually by going to the functions.php file. This will be very similar to turning on menus or widgets, as we've done before.

When adding to the functions.php file, try to comment as much as possible on what you're adding and why. Clearly defining why you're doing something a specific way will help others to understand your process and plan. Also, try to group elements with similar functionality together for easier consumption of the code later.

```
add_post_type_support( 'page', 'excerpt' );
```

The above function add_post_type_support accepts two parameters. The first is the post type we're modifying and the second is the functionality we're adding to that post type. In this case, we are adding excerpt support to pages. Seems simple enough, right? For more information on this function go to http://codex.wordpress.org/Function_Reference/add_post_type_support.

Once you add this to your functions.php file, you'll see a new Excerpt content area available in the Edit or Add New pages in the admin (**Figure 11.6**). If it's missing, go to Screen Options and turn it on. Now that we can add an excerpt we have to display it in the page template.

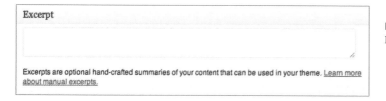

FIGURE 11.6
Excerpt content area.

Replace the following HTML:

```
<h2 class="tagline"><!-- THE EXCERPT --></h2>
```

with:

```
<?php if( get_the_excerpt() ) { ?>
  <h2 class="tagline"><?php echo get_the_excerpt(); ?></h2>
<?php } ?>
```

This outputs the following HTML:

```
<h2 class="tagline">I'm a huge fan of WordPress</h2>
```

It's vital to run the if statement before displaying anything to make sure that the user admin has added content to the excerpt area. We also have to echo the get_the_excerpt() function to disable the wpautop function, which automatically adds <p> tags around the content. We're inserting content in between <h2></h2> tags, so having unnecessary <p></p> tags wrapping everything will be a problem. Go to **http://codex.wordpress.org/Function_Reference/get_the_excerpt** for more information on get_the_excerpt();.

Content

By now you should be intimately familiar with the the_content() function, which displays everything in the content editor and should be utilized the same way as in previous chapters:

```
<?php the_content(); ?>
```

Custom Page Templates

The default page template we just created in page.php will be used to display all page content (including hierarchical post types). Basically, anytime a user visits a page, the page.php template structure is used to properly display that content. You have the option to define additional page templates to give the user admin more control over page layout. In this theme we'll also define a page template that has no sidebar and content that is "full width."

In page.php you'll see that the <aside></aside> tags are calling the aside sidebar. This is the same two-column layout we've used throughout the rest of the theme. For our full-width page template we'll remove the <aside> altogether and have the content take over the entire width of the page, making it a single-column layout.

The HTML structure has been laid out for you in page-full-width.php. Open this file and run through the above lesson, replacing all the static HTML with our dynamic WordPress calls and functions.

Defining a Custom Page Template

Now that we have a new page template, we actually have to provide a way for the user admin to assign pages to it. Throughout this book we've seen WordPress define rules and regulations in the way that we define functions, theme files, and activate theme support. Defining a custom page template requires us to adhere to certain rules, too.

At the top of the page-full-width.php file, insert the following commented-out PHP code:

```php
<?php
/*
Template Name: Full Width
*/
?>
```

Make sure that "Template Name: " is exactly as you see it above. "Full Width" will be the title of our page template and it will be displayed to the user admin. You can define multiple page templates in your theme, just make sure you choose unique names for each of them.

Once you add this to the top of the page-full-width.php page template, you'll see an option appear in the Edit or Add New page in the admin, seen in **Figure 11.7**. Every custom page template you define will show in this list.

FIGURE 11.7
Choosing a page template.

It's important to note that the page template will not alter the content of a page or even its inherent functionality. All we're doing is redefining how the content will be displayed to the user. In the full-width page template we're simply removing the aside and redefining the width of the main content area. This is a very simple change, but there is so much more that could be done.

Using Page Templates

Page templates can be used in a variety of ways. The main goal of a page template is to give the user admin control of the layout of a page. However, we can do so much more than that. We can use page templates to toggle functionality and more.

One issue with page templates is that you can't pick and choose which elements of the templates to turn on. This is better suited for custom values or optional post settings. In other words, you can't mix and match the ideas below, but this will at least get you off to a good start.

We can do some simple things like toggling comments (although this may be better done in the page settings) or author information.

Some of the more complex templates include:

Adding a photo gallery: Instead of using the featured image at the top, you can include a function or shortcode to pull in a photo gallery. You could always include this in the body of the text, but it's nice to be able to alter the layout so you can better associate the page elements.

Providing a walk-through: If you're selling services it can be helpful to create a path for visitors to walk through the services in a specific order. You can do this by adding Previous and Next buttons for sibling pages. For example, say you have a Services page and its child pages are ordered like this: Blogging, Social Media, SEO, and Web Design. When we're on the Social Media page, we'll see a link to Blogging and a link to SEO. The page template can call a function to find the previous and next sibling pages to create a walk-through.

Increasing conversion with a form: It's simple enough to include a form in the body of the content on a page. However, removing an element that's consistent throughout the site and replacing it with a form will make it more prominent. If you replace the featured image with a form at the top of a page using this page template, we'll likely see increased conversion on that page.

Including recent posts or other queries: It may make sense to include a list of recent posts or other queries with your page content. You can define a page template to pull a list of the most recent posts in the News category for any pages that are about the company. This way you're pairing static company information with dynamic posts.

Including Adsense or other ads: If you have a high-traffic page, you may want to include advertisements to increase revenue. This may not be desirable throughout your entire site, so setting up a page template that calls Adsense or another ad provider's code above and below the content will be a good solution.

These are just a few examples of page templates. Some others that weren't mentioned are simple HTML layout changes. We have two-column and single-column layouts, but maybe you need a three-column layout or want the sidebar above the content. There are hundreds of ways to configure your page layouts. It's a good idea to limit the number of page templates to less than ten for consistency and simplicity.

What's Next

We just discussed how to configure the page.php template page and create additional custom page templates. Next, we'll build out the Archive and Search Results pages. These pages require some specific functions in order to work correctly. One thing we'll pay close attention to is how to display the title of the archive or search result query so visitors have a better understanding of where they are.

Archive and
Search Results

12

The Archive and Search Results pages of your WordPress website are probably the most dynamic of all the template pages. The Loop will continue to power the data on these pages, which will make them easy to build out. We'll incorporate some specific functionality to help users understand where they are and what they're looking at.

What you're about to learn

- Archive page template best practices

- Search Results template best practices

- Constructing dynamic template page names using conditionals

- Displaying search queries in content

Archive and Search Results Page Layout

Once again we're not breaking out of our basic template structure all that much. We still have the header, aside, and footer. The content area pulls in a list of posts based on the user's location on the site. The Loop automatically generates the content list. So if we're viewing the Development archive page (**Figure 12.1**), we'll see only posts that are assigned to the Development category.

The Search Results page will have the same layout and functionality as the Archive page. We want to display what the user is searching for in the title of the Search Results page, and since it's easier to find what you're looking for without the featured images, we'll remove those images on the Search Results page as well. We'll add an additional search form as well, so users can search again and again until they find what they're looking for.

Archive Page Template

The Archive uses the archive.php page template file. This file displays archives from categories, tags, dates, and even authors. We learned in Chapter 3, "WordPress Template Hierarchy," that the template hierarchy comes into full effect with archives because of the specificity with which we can drill down with content.

By default the template hierarchy defaults to archive.php (which we're about to edit). If you want to create specific layouts for each type of archive, you can use the template files shown in **Table 12.1**.

TABLE 12.1 These template files control the layout of these types of archives.

FILE	ARCHIVE TYPE
category.php	Category archive
tag.php	Tag archive
author.php	Author archive
date.php	Date archive
taxonomy.php	Custom Taxonomy archive
archive-$posttype.php	Custom Post Type archive

For now we're working exclusively in archive.php, so these other template pages can use this as a foundation. When we're done, you can duplicate archive.php, rename it, and alter it for each specific archive type.

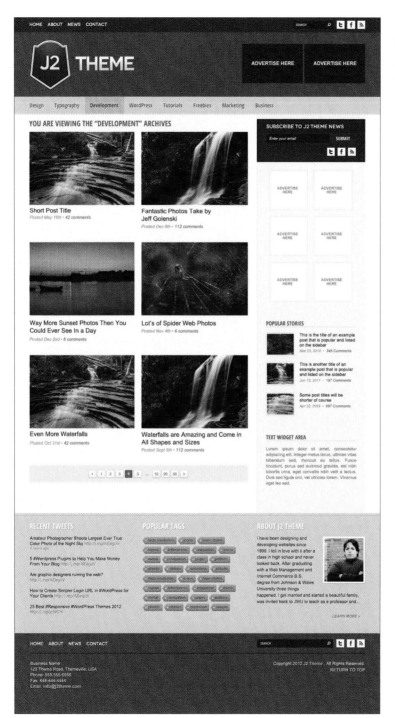

FIGURE 12.1
The Archive and Search Results page template.

Archive Header

The header is really the only thing that's changing here. In fact, if you look at the HTML structure from index.php and archive.php, we've removed the slider and replaced "RECENT NEWS" with "YOU ARE VIEWING THE 'Archives Title' ARCHIVES" (**Figure 12.2**). The two-column layout is the same, The Loop is the same, and so is the pagination at the bottom. Actually, that's not entirely true. Here we're displaying six posts, where on the home page we display four. Later in the book we'll look at advanced techniques to alter loop results with custom queries, so hold tight until then.

One of the key elements we want to generate dynamically is an informative title, which will then be included in the <h1> tag. Since we can't predict whether archive.php is being used to display daily, yearly, or category archives, we have to use some PHP to do some investigating. Once we determine what the user is viewing, we can display the appropriate page titles:

```php
<?php
  if ( is_day() )
    _e( 'You are viewing the ' . get_the_date() . ' daily archives' );
  elseif ( is_month() )
    _e( 'You are viewing the ' . get_the_date( 'F Y' ) . ' monthly archives' );
  elseif ( is_year() )
    _e( 'You are viewing the ' . get_the_date( 'Y' ) . ' yearly archives' );
  elseif ( is_author() )
    _e( 'You are viewing author archives' );
  else
    _e( 'You are viewing the "'. single_cat_title( '', false ) . '" Archives' );
?>
```

Copy the above code into the <h1></h1> tags on archive.php. This code runs through several archive types to determine where the user is, then displays the corresponding content. Let's break this down to get a better understanding of what's happening.

FIGURE 12.2 The Archive header.

IS_DAY()

First we create an if statement asking if is_day() returns true. (We'll cover conditionals in greater detail in later chapters.) The is_day() function tests to see if the page being viewed is a day-based archive page. A typical "day" archive has a URL such as http://localhost/ j2-theme/2012/05/15/. In this case, the URL prompts The Loop to pull only posts published on May 15, 2012, and the following code runs:

```
_e( 'You are viewing the ' . get_the_date() . ' daily archives' );
```

The code above echoes out the following HTML. (Note that the <h1></h1> tags are there because we placed this code in between them.)

```
<h1>You are viewing the May 15, 2012 daily archives</h1>
```

The get_the_date() function returns a value ready for echoing and, by default, it will be the Month, Day, Year format. For more information on is_day() and get_the_date(), go to http://wdgwp.com/is_day and http://wdgwp.com/get_the_date.

IS_MONTH()

The next line starts with elseif, which is basic PHP for saying "if the previous condition is not true, determine if this one is." Here we're testing the is_month() function, which, like the is_day() function, returns either true or false. A month archive URL looks like http://localhost/ j2-theme/2012/05/. Notice that the only thing missing from this example is the extra slash for the day.

```
_e( 'You are viewing the ' . get_the_date( 'F Y' ) . ' monthly archives' );
```

The above code outputs the following HTML:

```
<h1>You are viewing the May 2012 monthly archives</h1>
```

This time the get_the_date() function has been passed a parameter dictating the date format.

IS_YEAR()

At this point you should be seeing a pattern. Next up is the is_year() function, which tests against the yearly archives. The URL looks like http://localhost/j2-theme/2012/ and, in that case, the following code will run:

```
_e( 'You are viewing the ' . get_the_date( 'Y' ) . ' yearly archives' );
```

This code outputs the following HTML:

```
<h1>You are viewing the 2012 yearly archives</h1>
```

IS_AUTHOR()

The next test is to determine if we're currently on an author's Archive page. The URL looks like http://localhost/j2-theme/author/jfriedman/. Here, it would make sense to display the author's name and information, but I don't want to bombard you with too much too fast. For now, we'll simply use the following PHP code to echo a simple statement. If you're interested in going the extra mile, you can read about displaying author information outside The Loop at http://wdgwp.com/author_templates.

```
_e( 'You are viewing author archives' );
```

The statement above has no extra dynamic calls or functions, so it should be easy to predict what gets output.

```
<h1>You are viewing the author archives</h1>
```

> **BEST PRACTICE**
>
> You may have noticed by now that we often echo content using _e(), a WordPress function designed to allow for translating before the content is displayed. WordPress is used in many different languages, and your themes should be ready for that. It's good practice to use _e() and __() to translate your text before outputting it. For more information on this, go to http://wdgwp.com/_e and http://wdgwp.com/_2.

single_cat_title()

The else is PHP for "if everything else failed, do this." At this point it's safe to say that if it's not a day, month, year, or author archive, then it's a category. The URL typically looks like http://localhost/j2-theme/category/articles/ and, in this case, the following code:

```
_e( 'You are viewing the "'. single_cat_title( '', false ) . '" Archives' );
```

would output:

```
<h1>You are viewing the "Articles" archives</h1>
```

The single_cat_title() function is designed to return the title of the current category. The first parameter is what will precede the outputted content. Enter nothing here, because you don't want anything before the category name. The second parameter accepts only true or false, where true displays the data and false returns the value to be echoed or stored.

You can also implement this strategy specifically for is_tag() or any other taxonomy or archive-based page template.

The Archive Loop

Once again, The Loop isn't changing (for now), so you can use the code from previous chapters or copy the code below:

```
<?php if ( have_posts() ) : while ( have_posts() ) : the_post(); ?>
  <! -- PLACE HTML POST STRUCTURE HERE -->
<?php endwhile; else: ?>
  <p><?php _e( 'The archives you're looking for could not be found.' ); ?></p>
<?php endif; ?>
```

Notice that the article header defined previously is not in the loop. If it were, it would be duplicated for every iteration of a post.

Search Results

Did you know that in most cases a user can search a WordPress website, even if there's no search form available? WordPress uses a get var in the URL to initiate a search query. Whether you type "hello" into a search box or append ?s=hello to the end of your URL, you'll get the same result. WordPress runs a query for posts or pages that contain the word "hello." Fire up the search.php template file, which dictates the layout and functionality of the Search Results page (**Figure 12.3**).

FIGURE 12.3
The Search Results page.

Displaying the Search Query

Earlier in this chapter we displayed the Archive page title to help users better understand where they are and what they're viewing. On the Search Results page we want to display the query, or the string they searched for. This is helpful so they can clearly see what they typed into the search form, discover a typo or other error, and more easily decide whether a change needs to be made to get better results.

The output will be "YOU ARE SEARCHING FOR 'SEARCH QUERY'". There's no need to do a test with an if statement like we did with archive.php, because search.php is used for only one thing: displaying search results. All we have to do is echo out the above text while requesting the query input by the user. In the code below we utilize the _e() function and combine the static content with the get_search_query() function, which acts as the PHP $_GET['s'].

```php
<?php _e( 'You are searching for "' . get_search_query() . '"' );
```

> **■■■ NOTE**
>
> Anytime you see a ? at the end of a URL, it means that variables and values are being passed. This is common on Google Maps. The question mark starts the "getting" of variables and each one is deliminated by an ampersand. Here's an example: http://maps.google.com/maps?q=1+Police+Plaza,+New+York,+NY&hl=en where "q" probably stands for query and equals "1+Police+Plaza,+New+York,+NY". The next variable is "hl" and is separated from "q" with an "&" and equals "en". For more information about getting and posting variables, go to http://wdgwp.com/php-get and http://wdgwp.com/php-post.

In PHP the $_GET variable lets us collect the value of the variable we input as a parameter. Searching for "hello" creates a URL of http://localhost/j2-theme/?s=hello and $_GET['s'] equals "hello". The above PHP outputs:

```html
<h1>You are searching for "hello"</h1>
```

Next we want to display the search form again so the user can search again easily.

The Search Form

The search form should be displayed using the template tag get_search_form(). We'll go over exactly what it outputs in a second. (For future reference, if you want to customize the structure of the search form you can create a template file called searchform.php.) To get the basic foundation for the form, which you can alter to your liking, copy the code form wp-includes ➡ general-templates.php.

Just below the <h1></h1> tags used for displaying the query insert the get_search_form() function:

```php
<?php get_search_form(); ?>
```

This function outputs the following HTML:

```html
<form role="search" method="get" id="searchform" action="http://localhost/
      j2-theme/" >
  <div>
    <label class="screen-reader-text" for="s">Search for:</label>
    <input type="text" value="" name="s" id="s" />
    <input type="submit" id="searchsubmit" value="Search" />
  </div>
</form>
```

Once the search is performed, the value of the query is inserted as the value of the "value" attribute on the <input> tag. Here's an example for a search for "WordPress":

```html
<form role="search" method="get" id="searchform" action="http://localhost/
      j2-theme/" >
  <div>
    <label class="screen-reader-text" for="s">Search for:</label>
    <input type="text" value="wordpress" name="s" id="s" />
    <input type="submit" id="searchsubmit" value="Search" />
  </div>
</form>
```

This is a nice touch because if the user is searching something like "responsive web design" and noticed a spelling error, he wouldn't have to retype the entire query. For more information on get_search_form(), go to **http://wdgwp.com/get_search_form**.

The Loop

I bet you know what I'm about to say. That's right, we're not altering the structure of The Loop. The addition of ?s=query at the end of the URL prompts The Loop to display only posts that come up as a result of the search query. The one thing we will change is the error. Here especially, the error is extremely important. Nowhere else in the theme is it more likely that no posts will be found:

```php
<?php if ( have_posts() ) : while ( have_posts() ) : the_post(); ?>
  <! -- PLACE HTML POST STRUCTURE HERE -->
<?php endwhile; else: ?>
  <p><?php _e( 'Sorry, your search for "' . get_search_query() . '" returned
      no results.' ); ?></p>
<?php endif; ?>
```

If no posts are found, the following HTML will be output:

```html
<p>Sorry, your search for "Jesse Friedman Rocks!" returned no results.</p>
```

Once again we reiterate the search query, making it clear what the user is searching for.

the_excerpt();

In previous chapters we learned how to use the_excerpt to pull what's defined in the excerpt editor or the beginning of what's defined in the content editor. It also displays anything above the <!-- more --> tag, which you can read about at http://wdgwp.com/read_more.

Since the user is searching for something specific, we want to make it easier for him to find it. On the Search Results page, we've dumped the featured image. The featured image, while an important aspect of the design on the Archive page, doesn't add value to a search. The featured image of a post or page may not actually have anything to do with the content.

Instead of the featured image, we'll grab the excerpt and place it below the title. This helps the user find what he's looking for by providing a preview of the content on the page.

```php
<?php the_excerpt(); ?>
```

The above code should be inserted into The Loop below the title.

> ■■■ **NOTE**
>
> Now, it's up to you to replace the rest of the HTML in The Loop with Template Tags. We walked through every step of this task in previous chapters—think of it as a skill-building exercise.

What's Next

We just covered the creation of the Archive and Search Results page templates. You're ready for more already, huh? The next chapter will actually be an easy one: we'll be creating a 404 error template. This page template will be utilized anytime a 404 error is generated by the user entering an incorrect URL or visiting a recently removed page.

404 Error

A lot of strategy and thought goes into today's 404 pages. Instead of presenting the user with a worthless error message, we can actually provide a meaningful way of navigating the site. Instead of pointing a finger at the user that implies "you messed up," we can apologize for the inconvenience and assist him in finding what he's looking for.

What you're about to learn

- 404 industry best practices

- 404 template page creation

- Template tags and functions

404 Error

The 404 template page is used whenever anyone attempts to travel to a page, post, or other area of the site that doesn't exist. It could be the user's fault because he typed in something incorrectly, or it could be ours because we took down a page and didn't define a proper redirect. Either way, it's better to take the blame for it and move the user down the right path.

The 404 error template in **Figure 13.1** shows a lot of dynamic content being displayed but there's no 404 page in the admin. There's actually no content editor or any way to give the user admin access to the content on the 404. That's OK, because we don't have to predict anything on this template page. The user is here and we need to move him along.

In the template header there's a title, an error message, and a search form. The title will, for the first time in our theme build, be static. The message will be static as well. There's really no reason to pull in any dynamic content in these messages. Unlike the Search Results page where we could display the search query, there really isn't anything to display or help the user correct.

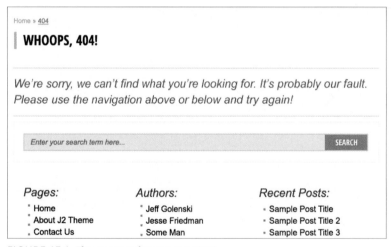

FIGURE 13.1 The 404 template page content.

Once we visit http://localhost/j2-theme/apples (which in my case, returns a 404), we'll start using the 404.php template page to display content. Once again the template is almost the same as the rest of the site. The header, sidebar, and footer are identical. They still require the necessary functions to display that content, for example, get_header().

404 Template Header

The title and error statement are pretty straightforward. You can replace the content at the top of the template with anything you prefer. I like to use a personal and humble statement when delivering an error.

```
<hl class="error">Whoops, 404!</hl>
<h2 class="tagline">We're sorry, we can't find what you're looking for. It's
      probably our fault. Please use the navigation above or below and try
      again!</h2>
```

The statement above lets the visitor know that there was an error on the site, but in a light-hearted and modest way. We take the blame for the mistake and let him know that he can easily continue the search. In fact, we will be providing navigation in addition to the header nav that is easily accessible, plus we'll provide a search form and a "sidebar" with a plethora of links and content below that. This way the user has the option to continue on the site as quickly as possible. Without this simple means of navigating and locating the content he's in search of, he'll probably be just another addition to the bounce rate.

The Search Form

We can display the search form exactly as we did in the previous chapter, using the get_search_form() function. The HTML output from this form is a bit different than what's displayed in the design. You can fix this by creating your own search template page or by hiding certain elements with CSS.

```
<?php get_search_form(); ?>
```

You can also replace the entire function with a slightly more static call to display the form. In the end, you use the function above or the code below—there's no wrong answer.

In 404.php replace the form content with the following code:

```
<form role="search" method="get" id="searchform" action="" >
  <input type="text" value="" name="s" id="s" />
  <input type="submit" id="searchsubmit" value="Search" />
</form>
```

There are only slight differences between this HTML markup and what follows. I've removed the content in the action="" attribute, along with the <label></label> and unnecessary <div></div> tags.

```
form role="search" method="get" id="searchform" action="http://localhost/
      j2-theme/" >
  <div>
    <label class="screen-reader-text" for="s">Search for:</label>
    <input type="text" value="" name="s" id="s" />
    <input type="submit" id="searchsubmit" value="Search" />
  </div>
</form>
```

Now the form won't function if we don't have a URL in the action attribute to post our variables to. The one problem is that we don't know what the URL of the site will be. So we need to input a dynamic WordPress call to display the URL in the attribute. Insert the bloginfo() function into the action attribute. Pass it a parameter of url to return the site's main URL.

```
<form role="search" method="get" id="searchform" action="<?php bloginfo(
      'url' ) ?>" >
  <input type="text" value="" name="s" id="s" />
  <input type="submit" id="searchsubmit" value="Search" />
</form>
```

Once we do this, the HTML output will be:

```
<form role="search" method="get" id="searchform" action="http://localhost/
      j2-theme/" >
  <input type="text" value="" name="s" id="s" />
  <input type="submit" id="searchsubmit" value="Search" />
</form>
```

Just like that, we have a working search form. You can now insert this code throughout your theme, convert it into a search template, or simply use it here.

Before we move on, here's an extra tip that's extremely helpful for larger sites with hundreds of posts. Many people don't know this, but you can search within a category simply by appending ?s=query at the end of the category URL. The benefit here is that you can implement search forms into archive template pages for easy searching of the specific category the user is currently viewing.

You could even go as far as creating a category drop-down above the form and then appending the category slug to the end of the action URL for searching within a category from anywhere on the site.

Another Dynamic Sidebar

I bet you thought we were done defining sidebars in our theme. Don't worry—this is good practice, and shaking things up will help you improve your WordPress skills. We defined our dynamic sidebars in previous chapters and, before you continue, I encourage you to go to functions.php, duplicate the register_sidebar(), and see if you can create a new sidebar on your own. If you get lost along the way, or break your site, have no fear. The code you're looking for is just ahead:

```
$j2theme_404 = array(
    'name'          => '404 Error Page',
    'id'            => 'fourohfour',
    'description'   => 'Widgets placed here will go on the 404 error page
        template',
    'before_widget' => '<div class="widget">',
    'after_widget'  => '</div>',
    'before_title'  => '<h3 class="widgettitle">',
    'after_title'   => '</h3>',
);
register_sidebar( $j2theme_404 );
```

It's good practice to plan your dynamic sidebars in advance but it's not always possible. In the past, the order of sidebar declarations could have an impact on widget placement. As of WordPress version 3.4 we no longer have this issue, so it's OK to reorder sidebars as you want. However, it is important to note that the order of the sidebars in the functions.php dictates their order on the Appearance → Widgets page.

Remember our best practices in function and variable declaration? Preface your names with something specific to your theme or plugin to prevent collisions with other code in the future. If you need a refresher on registering sidebars, revisit Chapter 9, "Dynamic Sidebars and Widgets," or go to http://wdgwp.com/register_sidebar.

Once you register the new sidebar, you can fill it with widgets. The design was really well done, so it's easy to display lots of widgets without complicating the site. All of the following widgets can be added to your new sidebar, but it's up to you and the user admin to fill them in:

- Pages

- Authors

- Recent posts

- Blog categories

- Monthly (archive)

We still have to display our sidebar in the 404 template page, so insert the following code below the search form:

```php
<?php dynamic_sidebar( '404 Error Page' ); ?>
```

We've just given the user admin a great deal more control over the 404 template page. It may seem like a lot of work for a page we hope visitors never find themselves on, but that's the point. We want to encourage them to stay on the site even when something goes wrong. Pithy and funny comments can keep them engaged, and giving them simple ways to navigate and continue through the site will likely turn a negative situation into a positive one.

What's Next

That wasn't too hard, right? It's good that you had a little breather, because next we're diving into another level of advanced coding. In Chapter 14, "Featured Images," we'll finally declare all our featured image sizes and distribute the correct calls throughout the theme.

Dear WordPress Recruit,

Now that you have an understanding of WordPress theme development, you're probably wondering how to expand your knowledge beyond what you've just learned. The best place to start is the WordPress Codex at http://wdgwp.com/codex. Maintained by the WordPress community (which now includes you), the codex covers many of the common WordPress APIs (functions, classes, and so on) organized into two primary categories: Function Reference (http://wdgwp.com/function_reference) and Template Tags (http://wdgwp.com/template_tags). This is all well and good, but what if you don't even know where to start?

The WordPress.org Support Forums at http://wdgwp.com/support are a great place to begin researching problems or questions. The WordPress Answers site on StackExchange (http://wdgwp.com/stack) is another excellent resource. Looking for general tutorials? Start with a trustworthy source, such as WPCandy (http://wdgwp.com/wpcandy) or iThemes (http://wdgwp.com/ithemes). Another often-overlooked resource is WordPress.tv, which hosts exclusively WordPress-related videos from WordCamps, WordPress meetups, and the like. Once your skills develop you'll be ready to delve into the core, and learn WordPress from itself.

Before you panic, know that this sounds far more intimidating than it actually is. WordPress Core is, thankfully, quite well organized. The bulk of its functionality is found in the wp-includes folder, while anything specific to administration is found in wp-admin.

One common area of frustration when first exploring wp-includes arises when you cannot locate a function you know exists. In this situation, there are three files to check: general-template.php, link-template.php, and pluggable.php. If that doesn't work, head over to http://wdgwp.com/phpxref, where you can search for the function in question. This resource, the WordPress Crossreference, is provided by Peter Westwood, a core contributor, and updates nightly to reflect the latest changes in WordPress.

It's also helpful to know that preceding the majority of function definitions is a comment block that details the function's intended use, accepted arguments, and expected results. Without needing to read a line of the function definition itself, you can gain insight into how to employ a given function.

I hope this discussion has alleviated some of your concern regarding advancing your WordPress skills by building on the foundation you gained from this book. As I hope you've learned, there are many reliable resources for learning WordPress, but none as detailed as the core itself.

Erick Hitter
ethitter.com | @ethitter

PART 4
Advanced

It's rare for me say that something I'm trying to accomplish in WordPress, even complex "outside the box" tasks can't, or shouldn't, be done. Most of the time on more "interesting" projects is spent researching how to do something the right way. In this section of the book, we are going to dive deeper into the WordPress API and learn how to accomplish some pretty complex tasks.

We will be going through examples like building a home page slider, or using shortcodes to augment content. While these specific examples may not translate to your exact project, the knowledge that these things can be done, and how to do them correctly, will save you a great deal of time later.

As a developer of any language or software, you should be able to manipulate or change what you learn to benefit your specific needs. Once again we'll be building a foundation, this time utilizing far more advanced functionality. This will give us greater control over our data and website.

Featured Images

We finally made it to the featured images chapter. There were several places in our theme that we just plopped in the the_post_thumbnail() function with no real direction, because I wanted to make sure you had a good foundation in theme development before we moved on to more advanced steps. Unfortunately, this means that we're doing things a little backwards, but now you should have no problem understanding everything in this chapter.

What you're about to learn

- How to register thumbnails for your theme

- How to creating multiple crop sizes

- The difference between hard and soft cropping

- How to display thumbnails by name in your theme

A Quick Recap

In previous chapters, we covered how to add theme support for post thumbnails (also called featured images), how to pull them into the theme, and how to upload them to a post. In case you've skipped around in the book or just want a refresher, here's what we've done so far:

```
add_theme_support( 'post-thumbnails' );
```

In the functions.php file we inserted the above code, which enabled the featured image on posts and pages. Then, in the template files, we put in the the_post_thumbnail() function, like so:

```
<?php the_post_thumbnail(); ?>
```

This outputs the following HTML, which basically takes the original image (assigned to that post as the featured image) and inserts it into the theme:

```
<img width="1200" height="2200" src="http://localhost/j2-theme/wp-content/
        uploads/2012/05/ch11-01-page-template.jpg" class="attachment-post-
        thumbnail wp-post-image" alt="ch11-01-page-template" title="ch11-01-
        page-template" />
```

The HTML above has width, height, alt, title, and class attributes, all of which are populated by the image panel in the library or on the Edit Post page. In most cases, we're using the featured image to display a small thumbnail in line with our posts. As you can see above, a 1200 × 2200px image will not do the job.

The next step is to locate all the sizes we need to define by looking through the theme design. Once we do that we can return to the functions.php and register those sizes.

Defining Thumbnail Sizes

On the home page there are two distinct featured image sizes, the slider (**Figure 14.1**) and the post thumbnail (**Figure 14.2**). In the sidebar there's a small thumbnail inline with the recent posts list (**Figure 14.3**). There's also a large featured image at the top of the post and page templates (**Figure 14.4**), and one on the full-width page template (**Figure 14.5**).

FIGURE 14.1 The slider image (530 × 215px).

FIGURE 14.2
The post thumbnail
(260 × 175px).

Who's Scared of Spiders? Not
these Photographers

Posted Dec 2 • 6 comments

POPULAR STORIES

This is the title of an example
post that is popular and listed
on the sidebar
Mar 23, 2010 • 345 Comments

FIGURE 14.3
The small thumbnail (65 × 50px).

FIGURE 14.4 The post and page templates featured image (530 × 95px).

FIGURE 14.5 The full-width page featured image (820 × 95px).

Once you locate the distinct thumbnails throughout the theme, document their location and size and decide whether you want to hard or soft crop them (Table 14.1).

TABLE 14.1 Organizing thumbnails.

Location	Width	Height	Crop
Home page slider	530px	215px	Hard
Post thumbnail	260px	175px	Hard
Small post thumbnail	65px	50px	Hard
Post and page featured image	530px	95px	Hard
Full-width featured image	820px	95px	Hard

Hard and Soft Cropping

The difference between hard and soft cropping is the actual cropping. In hard cropping, the image is resized until the maximum width or height is reached, then cropping occurs. In soft-cropping (also known as "box resizing"), the image is resized proportionally to fit inside your dimensions.

FIGURE 14.6 Image upload, full size (473 × 473px).

Here's an example of a hard crop. The original image seen in **Figure 14.6** is 473px wide and 473px high. In my functions.php, I defined an image size of 220px wide by 180px high and set crop to "true."

```
add_image_size( 'homepage-thumb', 220, 180, true );
```

You can see the resulting cropped image in **Figure 14.7**. The screenshot was resized from 473px wide to 220px wide. At that point it was cropped to 180px high. If the image were wider than it is tall, it would have been reduced to 180px high first, then cropped to 220px high. The hard crop ensures that the image is always the exact dimensions we define.

In many themes, a soft crop works just fine (**Figure 14.8**). However, our layout is very specific and requires the featured images to be a certain size. The problem with the hard crop is that we can't predict exactly how the image will crop. If there's a very tall photograph of people, we risk their heads getting clipped in the cropping process. The problem with the soft crop is that it doesn't maintain the image proportions, which could mean changes in the site layout.

FIGURE 14.7 Hard crop (220 × 180px).

FIGURE 14.8 Soft crop (180 × 180px).

Coding Image Sizes

In the functions.php file we'll define the names and specific sizes of each of the five thumbnails listed in Table 14.1. If we're defining a single thumbnail size we can use the set_post_thumbnail_size() function, which lets us define the width, height, and crop choice for a single featured image.

```
set_post_thumbnail_size( 100, 100, true );
```

The code above instructs WordPress to crop a thumbnail 100px × 100px every time an image is uploaded through the admin. We'll use a different function to accomplish the same thing. For more information on set_post_thumbnail(), go to **http://wdgwp.com/set_post_thumbnail_size**.

In the functions.php below the add_theme_support('post-thumbnails') function, copy the code below:

```
add_image_size( 'slider', 530, 215, true );
add_image_size( 'post-thumb', 260, 175, true );
add_image_size( 'sm-post-thumb', 65, 50, true );
add_image_size( 'page-featured-image', 530, 95, true );
add_image_size( 'fullwidth-featured-image', 820, 95, true );
```

The add_image_size() function accepts four parameters. The first is the name of the thumbnail we're creating. The second and third are the width and height, respectively. The last parameter is a true or false statement that indicates whether or not to hard crop. In the theme, we're hard cropping all the featured images.

Note that in order to maintain the theme's design and layout, every featured image must be at least 820px wide by 215px high. If an image is not at least as wide or tall as the largest dimensions we define, then WordPress will be unable to resize it correctly. If we upload an image that is 820px wide but 105px tall, the "fullwidth-featured-image" will resize fine. However, the "slider" will not: its final cropped size will be 530px × 105px. This is a common practice, and it's a good idea to mention this in any documentation you provide with the theme.

With the image dimensions defined in the functions.php file, let's run through an example. Say you upload example.png, which is 1100px × 700px. Once the image is uploaded, WordPress automatically resizes and crops (if necessary) all versions of it. The images will be renamed and stored in the Uploads folder, which is located in wp-content and has subfolders based on the year and month of the upload. Table 14.2 shows a list of the images that now exist in wp-content/uploads/2012/05/.

TABLE 14.2 Example image in all sizes.

NAME	WIDTH	HEIGHT	RELATIONSHIP
example.png	1100px	700px	Original
example-65x50.png	65px	50px	sm-post-thumb
example-150x150.png	150px	150px	Default resize
example-260x175.png	260px	175px	post-thumb
example-300x190.png	300px	190px	Default resize
example-530x95.png	530px	95px	page-featured-image
example-530x215.png	530px	215px	slider
example-820x95.png	820px	95px	fullwidth-featured-image
example-1024x651.png	1024px	651px	Default resize

The resizing and renaming occurs immediately after you upload the image to WordPress. The images tagged as "Default resize" under relationship are images that are resized based on the default settings in Settings → Media in the WordPress admin. Figure 14.9 shows the media settings, which can be changed by the user admin and are typically used in the body content of posts and pages.

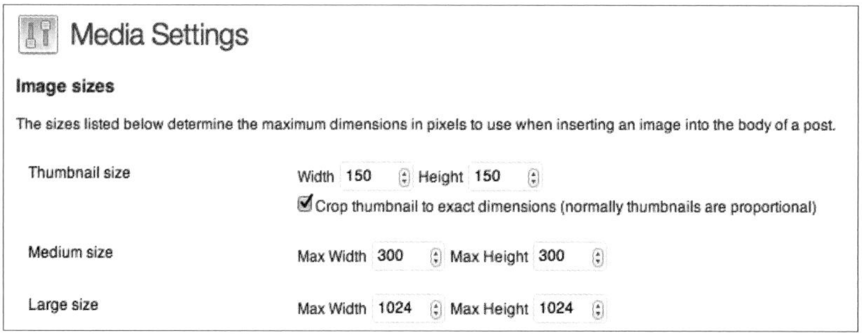

FIGURE 14.9 Media settings.

Displaying Featured Images

Displaying featured images is relatively simple now that we have defined them in our functions.php file. The next step is to go back to the page templates (index.php, archive.php, page.php, page-full-width.php, and single.php) and add the name of the thumbnail to the the_post_thumbnail() function.

On the home page, the slider will be defined in greater detail later. For now, insert 'slider' into the the_post_thumbnail() function like so:

```php
<?php the_post_thumbnail( 'slider' ); ?>
```

This outputs the following HTML:

```html
<img width="530" height="215" src="http://localhost/j2-theme/wp-content/
    uploads/2012/05/example-530x215.png" class="attachment-slider
    wp-post-image" alt="example" title="example" />
```

Notice the hard-coded width and height attributes. This will cause us problems later when we want the site to be responsive. The rest of the <img> is pretty straightforward and the src="" is pulling the exact image we needed.

We need to duplicate these steps for all the other the_post_thumbnail() calls. I've laid out a little plan of attack for you below.

INDEX.PHP → SLIDER

PHP

```php
<?php the_post_thumbnail( 'slider' ); ?>
```

HTML

```
<img width="530" height="215" src="http://localhost/j2-theme/wp-content/
    uploads/2012/05/example-530x215.png" class="attachment-slider
    wp-post-image" alt="example" title="example" />
```

INDEX.PHP → THE LOOP AND ARCHIVE.PHP → THE LOOP

PHP

```
<?php the_post_thumbnail( 'post-thumb' ); ?>
```

HTML

```
<img width="260" height="175" src="http://localhost/j2-theme/wp-content/
    uploads/2012/05/example-260x175.png" class="attachment-post-thumb
    wp-post-image" alt="example" title="example" />
```

SINGLE.PHP → THE HEADER AND SINGLE.PHP → THE HEADER

PHP

```
<?php the_post_thumbnail( 'page-featured-image' ); ?>
```

HTML

```
<img width="530" height="95" src="http://localhost/j2-theme/wp-content/
    uploads/2012/05/example-530x95.png" class="attachment-page-featured-
    image wp-post-image" alt="example" title="example" />
```

PAGE-FULL-WIDTH.PHP → THE HEADER

PHP

```
<?php the_post_thumbnail( 'fullwidth-featured-image' ); ?>
```

HTML

```
<img width="820" height="95" src="http://localhost/j2-theme/wp-content/
    uploads/2012/05/example-820x95.png" class="attachment-fullwidth-
    featured-image wp-post-image" alt="example" title="example" />
```

CUSTOM WIDGETS OR OTHER AREAS

PHP

```php
<?php the_post_thumbnail( 'sm-post-thumb' ); ?>
```

HTML

```html
<img width="65" height="50" src="http://localhost/j2-theme/wp-content/
    uploads/2012/05/example-65x50.png" class="attachment-sm-post-thumb
    wp-post-image" alt="example" title="example" />
```

With replacements to all the template files in place, our featured images should be displaying correctly. One way that WordPress continues to make our lives easier is in the class attribute on the <img> tags. If you were keen enough to notice, WordPress actually appends a custom class name based on the featured image function given name, as shown in **Table 14.3**.

TABLE 14.3 Featured image name and appended CSS class.

Given Name	Class appended by WordPress
slider	attachment-slider
post-thumb	attachment-post-thumb
page-featured-image	attachment-page-featured-image
fullwidth-featured-image	attachment-fullwidth-featured-image
sm-post-thumb	attachment-sm-post-thumb

This is a nice little added benefit, making it far easier to target featured images anywhere in the theme. It's also one more reason to be semantic in our naming conventions.

What's Next

Correctly coding and displaying the featured images adds a lot of functionality to our theme. This was a good stepping-stone into more advanced WordPress coding. Up next we'll look at how to query specific posts, filter the loop, and create a slider. Chapter 15, "Custom Fields," takes you up a level in advanced development, but at the same time helps you reap a lot of rewards.

Custom Fields

Before the existence of custom post types, custom fields were the tool of choice to enhance out-of-the-box WordPress functionality. I once built a 23,000-page directory using WordPress and custom fields. They give you precise control over metadata for specific posts and pages.

Now that we have custom post types and greater control over data tied to posts and pages, custom fields are used primarily for specific functions, such as toggling elements on posts or pages, showing or hiding content, and so on. In our theme we'll be using custom fields to set the URL of our home page slider.

What you're about to learn

■ How to set custom fields in a post

■ How to display all custom fields on a post

■ How to use custom field data for a specific purpose

Setting Custom Fields

Custom fields are handled by key/value pairs. When a user admin defines a new custom field, he names the new metadata with a key and then sets the value to be associated with it. A simple example could be storing colors. The key would be called "colors" and the value would be "blue." One key can be used multiple times on a single post. So you can set blue, red, and yellow to the "colors" key. When you call the key to display, WordPress returns an array of values associated with the specific key. We'll get into that later. For more info on custom fields, go to http://wdgwp.com/Custom_Fields.

> **BEST PRACTICE**
>
> As discussed previously, custom naming conventions to reduce conflict is important in functions. It's also important with custom values. Make sure you create custom value keys with a custom prefix like j2theme_color.

To set a custom field, go to the bottom of the Edit Post page and locate the Custom Fields section (**Figure 15.1**). If you don't see the Custom Fields section, go to Screen Options at the top of the page and toggle Custom Fields "on" (**Figure 15.2**).

FIGURE 15.1 Custom Fields section of the Edit Post page.

FIGURE 15.2 Screen Options toggle for Custom Fields.

Here you'll see two fields. The left field is labeled "name." Here you'll put the name of the custom field (that is, the key). The right field is the value. For now, enter "blue" (**Figure 15.3**). Once your fields are set, click Add Custom Field. This sets your custom field key and value pair. It's always good to click Update or Save at the top of the post to make sure everything saves accurately.

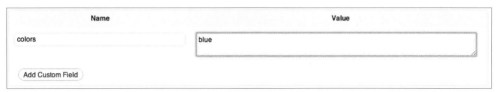

FIGURE 15.3 Adding the first custom field.

Now that you've created your first custom value, you'll see a different layout in the Custom Field section. **Figure 15.4** shows a drop-down menu from which you can choose existing keys. If you want to add a new custom field, you can click the Add New text below the drop-down. You'll also notice that your custom field has been saved and now appears above the Add New section.

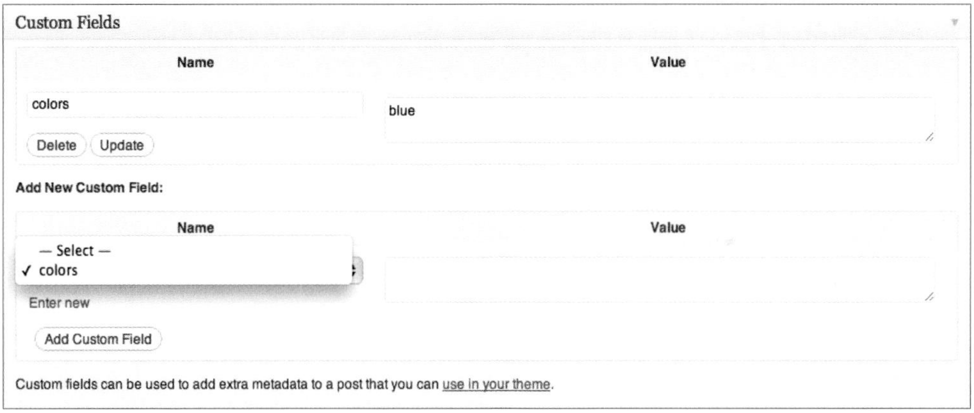

Custom Fields

Name	Value
colors	blue

Delete Update

Add New Custom Field:

Name	Value
— Select — ✓ colors Enter new	

Add Custom Field

Custom fields can be used to add extra metadata to a post that you can use in your theme.

FIGURE 15.4 Adding additional custom fields.

This was a very basic example to show you how to save data in the Custom Fields section. Remember that these key/value pairs are specific to each post; none of this data is global. Also, it's important to note that this data is saved as a string, so if you want to, you can save HTML markup in the values field as well. If you're building your theme for a specific person or company, you can create these custom values on behalf of the User Admin. Otherwise, it's important to create documentation on how to implement custom values and how they'll be used in the theme.

Displaying Custom Fields

As with other aspects of WordPress, there are several ways to accomplish a single task. With custom fields, you can display a list of all the values saved to a single post. You can also request specific values by passing keys as a parameter. Let's start by displaying a list of all of our favorite colors using the the_meta() function. You can visit the codex for more info on the the_meta() function at http://wdgwp.com/the_meta.

Let's assume I've added blue, red, and yellow as values under my "colors" key. When I add the following WordPress Template Tag:

```php
<?php the_meta(); ?>
```

to my loop it, outputs an HTML list of all my custom fields keys and their values.

```html
<ul class='post-meta'>
  <li><span class='post-meta-key'>colors:</span> blue, red, yellow</li>
</ul>
```

While this function makes it easy to display all my keys and their values, it really doesn't provide a great deal of control over the data.

Controlling Custom Fields and Their Values

Let's dig deeper into custom fields and create an example where we need to manipulate a specific custom value as a variable. Suppose the user admin has created a page where he is accepting donations to his favorite charity. Let's say his goal is to reach $1,000 in donations. You can set the donations goal and current dollar figure as custom fields, then subtract the difference so users will know how much more is needed to reach the goal.

Start by setting 1000 as the value for the "goal" key. Then set 450 as the "current_figure" key. In this case the goal is to reach $1,000 and we've already accepted $450 in donations. Your post custom fields area should look like **Figure 15.5**.

With the custom fields set, we now need to store the data from the custom fields in variables, perform an equation on those variables, and display them. For the purposes of this example, we're temporarily putting this code at the end of The Loop in the page.php template. We'll remove it later as it's just a teaching example and won't be included in the new theme.

FIGURE 15.5 Custom fields donations.

> **BEST PRACTICE**
>
> In the example in this chapter, a best practice would be to create a new custom page template to give us greater control over the appearance of the donations section. For more information on creating custom page templates, refer to Chapter 11, "Page."

In order to manipulate specific values, we need to request them. The the_meta() function won't work here. Instead, we'll use the get_post_custom_values() function, which lets us pass a key as a parameter and get back an array of values. For more information on this function, go to http://wdgwp.com/get_post_custom_values. Since we're "getting" the values, we need to save them to a variable. The following PHP code requests the two values we need and stores them in variables:

```php
<?php
    $j2theme_donation_goal = get_post_custom_values( 'goal' );
    $j2theme_current_figure = get_post_custom_values( 'current_figure' );
?>
```

It's important that the parameters are exactly the same as the key names set in the post. Once we have the data saved as variables we can manipulate them as we see fit. Remember that keys can hold multiple values, so we will always receive an array. If there's only one value, we'll get an array with a single index.

```php
<?php
    $j2theme_donation_diff = $j2theme_donation_goal[0]
        - $j2theme_current_figure[0];
?>
```

The next line creates a new variable called $j2theme_donation_diff that equals $j2theme_donation_goal[0] minus $j2theme_current_figure[0]. We appended [0] to the end of the arrays to grab the first element in the array.

Now we can actually display the data. The next line echoes an <h1> tag, stating how far we are from our fundraising goal:

```php
<?php
  echo '<h1>We are only $' . $j2theme_donation_diff . ' away from our $' .
        $j2theme_donation_goal[0] . ' goal. Donate Today!</h1>';
?>
```

In four lines of code we can create some pretty significant functionality. Now the user admin just needs to go to the Donate page and update the current_figure custom field, and the page will update with the new figures. The complete PHP code seen below should be added to the page.php in The Loop (again, just for this example):

```php
<?php
    $j2theme_donation_goal = get_post_custom_values( 'goal' );
    $j2theme_current_figure = get_post_custom_values( 'current_figure' );
    $j2theme_donation_diff = $j2theme_donation_goal[0]
        - $j2theme_current_figure[0];
    echo '<h1>We are only $' . $j2theme_donation_diff . ' away from our $' .
        $j2theme_donation_goal[0] . ' goal. Donate Today!</h1>';
?>
```

This outputs the following HTML:

```
<h1>We are only $550 away from our $1000 goal. Donate Today!</h1>
```

If you wanted to have some real fun with this, you could create a gauge or other diagram and use jQuery and these two values to create a graphical representation of how far we are from the goal.

Home Page Slider URL

Our theme doesn't require anything this complex. We'll be using a custom field to house the URL for our home page slider. Before we continue, I challenge you to complete the next step without reading the rest of this chapter. The task is to add a custom field to the slider posts we've created to generate the home page slider. You'll need to create a custom field with a key of "j2theme_url" and a value of "http://localhost/sample-page" (this URL is only temporary and should be modified for your site). Then display that URL in The Loop (you'll learn how to use the URL below).

Give it a shot on your own. If you can't get it, go ahead and finish this chapter. I'll walk you through it now. Start by adding a new custom field in a post. The key will be "url" and the value will be "http://localhost/sample-page," as seen in **Figure 15.6.**

Name	Value
j2theme_url	http://localhost/sample-page
Delete Update	

FIGURE 15.6 URL custom field.

For now we'll put the following PHP code into the single.php file. This will be for testing only; in the next chapter, we'll place it in The Loop for the slider (at that point you can remove it from single.php):

```php
<?php
  $j2theme_slider_url = get_post_custom_values( 'j2theme_url' );
  echo $j2theme_slider_url[0];
?>
```

This should be pretty straightforward. We call the get_post_custom_values() function, pass it the parameter of "j2theme_url," and store what it returns in the variable $j2theme_slider_url. Then we echo the first value in the array. This outputs the URL we saved in the custom field "http://localhost/sample-page."

That's it. Pretty simple, right?

What's Next

In the next chapter we'll tie what we learned in Chapter 14, "Featured Images," in with custom values and WP_Query() to create our slider. WP_Query() is a powerful WordPress class that lets us manipulate and change The Loop. This gives us greater control over the exact posts that get displayed.

Dear Future WordCamp Speaker,

It's been a wild three years since I made WordPress the center of my attention. When I first dabbled with WordPress in 2006, I characterized it merely as a "promising" open source blogging platform. I had no idea that five years later it would become the focal point on which I'd build a web agency. WordPress has made me a better developer and a better software citizen, provided me with an international community and network, and has even been the source of friendships that extend well beyond the software.

Here are a few of the guiding principles I try to impart when I teach WordPress:

It's not "can" WordPress do that, but "how" and "should" it. When it comes to building a website or web application, WordPress' core methods for building objects and relationships (post types, taxonomies, and metadata), ubiquitous hooks for changing default behavior, and full access to PHP and MySQL can certainly meet the requirements. The real question is how to do it, and given the cost of choosing WordPress, whether or not it should be done with WordPress. Sometimes a different tool is a better fit, but I guarantee WordPress can do it. Challenge yourself to figure out how.

Contribute something, and put your name on it. Nothing will challenge you to give a project your all like attaching your personal reputation to it. Consider developing a plugin or theme and releasing it to the official WordPress plugin or theme repository. Alternatively, help patch some core bugs or feature requests using WordPress Trac, or get involved in a WordPress meetup or WordCamp.

Embrace, don't fear, the core codebase. Relying on the codex and Google searches for solving unique problems with WordPress is like trying to tune a car's performance without ever looking under the hood.

Use an integrated development environment (IDE). True PHP IDEs like NetBeans, phpStorm, and phpDesigner offer code autocompletion to help you discover and remember WordPress functions and their arguments, inline WordPress function documentation (via PHPDoc support), and a means to easily jump to function and class declarations in core code to study them.

Combine these tips with a mentor who can offer feedback on your code, and you'll be on your way to being a rock star.

Jake Goldman
10up.com | @jakemgold

WP_Query()

Until now we've used the user location on the site to dictate what posts to show in The Loop. The Loop automatically detects whether a user is on the Articles category, for example, then displays only posts in that category. This is a really helpful function and it makes it easy to display content. However, there are times when you might want more freedom and control over the content.

You may want to display posts but exclude everything from a specific category or maybe you want to show only posts from the previous month. More simply, you might want to show a different number of posts than what is set in the default settings.

Our theme has a home page slider, which we have yet to code out. In this case we need to display up to five posts from a specific category. This chapter will show you how to use WP_Query(), a powerful class that lets you set the specific categories and number of posts to display.

What you're about to learn

- Solutions for filtering the basic loop

- An in-depth look at WP_Query()

- Alternatives and best practices for querying specific data

- Ideas for improving or building on a theme with WP_Query()

Getting Started with Custom Queries

There are many reasons why you might want to create custom queries to filter a request for posts or other content. WP_Query() lets you tap right into the WordPress API and filter, change, or modify The Loop however you want. But before we jump into WP_Query(), let's look at a quick and easy alternative.

query_posts()

The function below is an outdated way to alter The Loop:

```php
<?php query_posts() ?>
```

There are several drawbacks to using query_posts(), but knowing how it works will enable you to reverse engineer other developers' code. You may see query_posts() in action a lot because it's a simple way to alter The Loop. For example, let's say you want to display all the posts from your Tutorials category from the year 2011.

To request posts from a specific category and year we need to alter The Loop. This function call goes directly above the first line of The Loop and changes the parameters of The Loop by passing those values through query_posts():

```php
<?php query_posts( 'cat=8&year=2011' ); ?>
```

There are many parameters you can pass to this function—everything from author ID to publication date to specific post IDs. You can even decide how you want to order the posts (by date, alphabetically, or otherwise).

The query_posts() function accepted 'cat=8&year=2011' as parameters. This is technically a single PHP parameter because it's in one "set." However, we're separating specific filtering parameters with the "&" so we can pass multiple values in one parameter. When this is placed above The Loop, The Loop definition is redefined and no longer dependent on the user's location on the site. This requires The Loop to return posts that are posted in category 8 and published in 2011.

One drawback to using query_posts() is that it can potentially redefine all the loops on the template page. In the index.php template file we'll require a loop for the slider and an additional loop for the recent content. We'll need to reset the query parameters after The Loop by inserting the code below, immediately after the end of The Loop:

```php
<?php wp_reset_query(); ?>
```

For more information on query_posts() and wp_reset_query()visit the codex at http://
wdgwp.com/query_posts and here http://wdgwp.com/wp_reset_query.

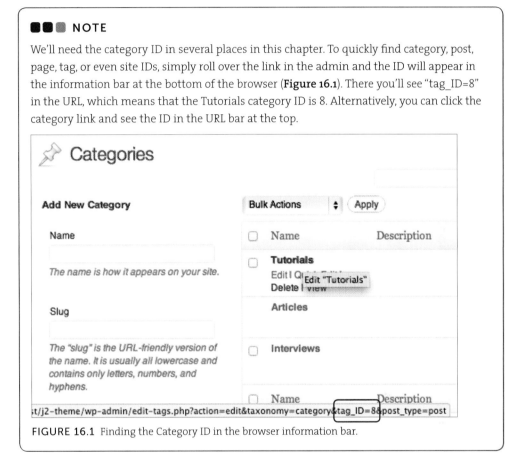

■■■ NOTE

We'll need the category ID in several places in this chapter. To quickly find category, post,
page, tag, or even site IDs, simply roll over the link in the admin and the ID will appear in
the information bar at the bottom of the browser (**Figure 16.1**). There you'll see "tag_ID=8"
in the URL, which means that the Tutorials category ID is 8. Alternatively, you can click the
category link and see the ID in the URL bar at the top.

FIGURE 16.1 Finding the Category ID in the browser information bar.

A BASIC WP_QUERY()

A better solution to the problem is to use the WP_Query() class. It requires a little more
work but there are several advantages, many of which we'll cover shortly. The great thing
about WP_Query() is that it can be used to create simple queries to extremely complex queries. You can read more about it and see the full list of parameters at http://wdgwp.com/
WP_Query.

Let's use WP_Query() to replicate the same results as above. The process is pretty much the same. Above the loop we'll define a series of parameters that will change the output of the loop:

```php
<?php
  // The Query
  $the_query = new WP_Query( 'cat=8&year=2011' );

  // The Loop
  if ( $the_query->have_posts() ) : while ( $the_query->have_posts() ) :
      $the_query->the_post();
?>

    <li><a href="<?php the_permalink(); ?>"><?php the_title(); ?></a></li>

<?php
  endwhile; endif;

  // Reset Post Data
  wp_reset_postdata();
?>
```

The first thing we need to do is define a new instance of the WP_Query class, like so: $the_query = new WP_Query($args). Once we define a new instance of the class we can pass it the parameters and call it in our loop later. For more info on PHP classes, go to http://wdgwp.com/php_classes.

Our loop gets modified a bit but the basic idea is still there. Inside the loop we continue to use our HTML mixed with Template Tags to create a list of post titles and links.

At the end of the code we close the while loop and reset the global $post data with the wp_reset_postdata() function. You can read more about that at http://wdgwp.com/wp_reset_postdata.

Once the code runs, it returns a list of posts, their titles, and links wrapped in <li></li> tags that reside only in the Tutorials category and were published in 2011. It was a little more work to create our loop in this fashion, but in the end, it's a better practice and makes for better, more scalable themes.

Slider

We'll populate our home page slider with HTML from a WP_Query() loop. Early on we decided to use a specific category called "Slider" to hold all our slider posts. (Remember that this isn't the best solution for this task, but defining custom post types is out of the scope of this book.) In the admin I created a new category with the ID of "9." The other element to the slider is that we want to feature a maximum of five posts at a time. So, in our WP_Query() parameters we need to define the category ID 9 and limit the number of results to five. Above, we passed our parameters together as a string. This time we'll create an array and then pass it to the WP_Query() class. This makes it easier to conceptualize our parameters and keeps things better organized.

Open the index.php template file and in the slider HTML (which is defined for you) place the following PHP code:

```php
<?php
  // The Query
  $j2theme_slider_param = array (
    'cat' => '9',
    'posts_count' => '5',
    );


  $the_query = new WP_Query( $j2theme_slider_param );


  // The Loop
  if ( $the_query->have_posts() ) : while ( $the_query->have_posts() ) :
      $the_query->the_post();
?>
    <a href="<?php $j2theme_slider_url = get_post_custom_values('url');
        echo $j2theme_slider_url[0];?>" title="<?php the_title(); ?>"><?php
        the_post_thumbnail('slider'); ?></a>
  <?php
  endwhile; endif;


  // Reset Post Data
    wp_reset_postdata();
?>
```

Let's go through this step by step. The first thing to do is define the array, $j2theme_slider_
param, which will hold our parameters' definitions. Remember, it's good practice to preface
your variables with a custom prefix. The format of the array declaration is something you'll
have to get used to, as it's just basic PHP format. You can learn more about defining PHP
arrays at **http://wdgwp.com/php_arrays**. In the array we're assigning '9' to 'cat' and '5' to
'posts_count'. These parameter names are set by WordPress. For a full list of what you can
define in WP_Query() go to **http://wdgwp.com/WP_Query_params**.

With the array complete the next step is to pass it to the new instance of WP_Query().
Immediately following $the_query declaration is our modified loop. Inside The Loop the
structure of the HTML is based on the requirements for the jQuery-based Nivo Slider, which
asks for wrapping the featured image in an <a> tag. Notice the use of the get_post_custom_
values() function, which we use to pull the URL custom value set by the user admin. (Refer
back to Chapter 15, "Custom Fields.")

The last steps are to close the while loop and reset the post data. This freshly defined loop
returns a maximum of five posts from the Slider category, displays its featured image ("slider"
size), title, and "url" custom field. Once this HTML is output (see below) the Nivo Slider code
does the rest of the work, configuring the jQuery and functionality of the slider:

```
<a href="http://jesserfriedman.com" title="About Jesse Friedman"><img
    width="530" height="215" src="http://localhost/j2-theme/wp-content/
    uploads/2012/05/jesse-530x215.png" class="attachment-slider wp-post-
    image" alt="Image of Jesse Friedman" title="About Jesse Friedman" />


<a href="http://worldclassdesigner.com" title="About Jeff Golenski"><img
    width="530" height="215" src="http://localhost/j2-theme/wp-content/
    uploads/2012/05/jeff-530x215.png" class="attachment-slider wp-post-
    image" alt="Image of Jeff Golenski" title="About Jeff Golenski" />
```

Now that the slider is properly defined, the user admin can add as many posts to the Slider
category as she pleases. The user admin can define slides as "on" or "off" by setting them to
draft or published, and reorder them by changing the publication dates on the posts.

Using Custom Queries

We just built our home page slider by creating an alternative loop. This was a great example of the WP_Query() because it covered all the basics and was rather simple to do. In the future, you can use WP_Query() to do a variety of things and add really complex functionality to your site. Let's take a look at some fun ways to use what we just learned. These examples show only the changes made to the parameters array. The rest of the loop would change based on the necessary HTML structure.

Featured Author

Imagine you have a large blog or article-based website with dozens of staff contributors and guest writers. One thing you don't want to do is lose access to the founder and head writer. Maybe they only contribute once a week or once a month. It'd be easy for their articles to get lost in the mix.

We can use WP_Query() to define an author ID and pull posts from only the specific head writer. Or if you have multiple featured authors, you can pass several author IDs. This is a great solution to featured content on the site's home page. Place your new loop in the home template file and you'll be showcasing your head authors above everything else:

```
$parameters = array (
   'author' => '1',
   'posts_count' => '3',
);
```

The above code displays the three most recent posts from the author with ID 1. You can also call multiple authors, as shown in the following example:

```
$parameters = array (
   'author' => '1,5,8',
   'posts_count' => '3'
);
```

In this case all you have to do is place commas between the IDs and the most recent posts from these authors will display. It's important to note that you're not getting the three most recent posts from each author. Instead the query finds the three most recent posts from any of the authors. So, if author 5 wrote the last three posts, only hers would be displayed.

Company Blog

Another common example would be excluding a specific category from the template page. Let's say your company has a blog with several categories, one of which is specifically geared to investors. To everyone else these articles may be irrelevant or even boring. You could use the cat parameter to list only the IDs you want to show, but that's a lot of work. Instead you can just state which category you want to exclude:

```
$parameters = array (
   'cat' => '-7'
);
```

We still use the "cat" parameter this time, but notice the "-" symbol before the number 7. This tells the query that we need to "minus" or exclude category 7. You can use the minus symbol in front of many values in WP_Query().

Locations Custom Post Types

We haven't built custom post types but in the future you might well be doing a lot of them. You might have a site utilizing custom post types to create locations. In this case you can use WP_Query() to display all the locations and sort them alphabetically:

```
$parameters = array (
   'post_type' => 'locations',
   'orderby' => 'title',
   'order' => 'ASC',
);
```

The 'post_type' parameter can accept inherent post types like "post" or "page." It can also accept developer-defined custom post types like "locations." Next, define the "orderby" parameter, which has several choices like title, ID, date, comment count, and more. The last parameter is "Order," which is either "ASC" (a,b,c or 1,2,3) or "DESC" (c,b,a or 3,2,1).

What's Next

We just covered WP_Query() pretty extensively, but there are many more ways to use this class. The best way to figure out what can be done is to imagine using or filtering content and reverse engineering it. Take a close look at http://wdgwp.com/WP_Query_params and you'll get a good idea of how far you can take this powerful class. In the next chapter, we'll create basic functions, define shortcodes, and take some time to organize our functions.php file.

Dear WordPress Padawan,

One of the most difficult parts of building a WordPress theme is providing ways for users with different requirements to customize it. It's just like customizing a family van by adding an extra seat or a roof rack. Similarly, WordPress offers four interesting methods to prepare a theme for extensibility—filters, action hooks, pluggable functions, and child themes—and each one adds possibilities to the mix.

Filters allow the user admin to alter the way content is output, either by prepending or appending extra content, or by completely overwriting it with different content. For example, you can use plugins to add social-sharing buttons at the beginning or end of the post. In other words, plugins usually filter the post content, and either prepend or append the buttons.

Action hooks provide an insertion point to inject HTML into a page, and each theme includes a bunch of them. One of the most popular hooks, wp_head, lets users insert HTML into the <head> tag of a page. I highly recommend that this hook be added in each theme.

Pluggable functions are simply functions that are first checked for their existence using PHP's function_exists(). If you create pluggable functions, users can easily and safely redefine them with custom functions.

Maybe you're already familiar with the child theme concept, which is basically creating a theme that uses code and markup from another theme. A child theme pretty much encompasses the options offered by other alternatives. Still, that doesn't mean you should discard filters or pluggable functions, because a child theme can quickly override a code segment across the entire site.

In short, by adding these extensible and modifiable mechanisms, your theme will be ready to go in any direction your users want it to go.

Finally, if you're getting serious about WordPress development, you should start checking WordPress' internal code for functions. Some IDEs—like Aptana Studio 3—let you Cmd+click on a function name to open its declaration. In WordPress, the internal code in WordPress is well-documented, explaining what it does, what arguments it admits, and what it returns. Best of all, you'll find the code in context, right at the tip of your fingers.

Elio Rivero
themify.me | @eliorivero

Shortcodes and Custom Functions

PHP functions can't be implemented in content, widgets, and many other areas, so pulling in a list of recent posts, galleries, ads, and other things can be difficult. Shortcodes are predefined functions in a simple format that you can set to let user admins call PHP functions in their content.

You can also create and then later call your own custom functions. There are countless reasons to write your own functions into your WordPress theme. Anytime you implement the same code over and over, it makes sense to pull it out, make it a function, and then call in your theme. Remember that it's good practice to remove duplicate code as much as possible.

What you're about to learn

- How shortcodes work

- How to write custom shortcodes

- How to implement shortcodes in content and widgets

- How to write and implement custom functions

- How to use conditional statements to determine when to incorporate an element

Shortcodes

Shortcodes empower user admins to perform functions that they would otherwise be unable to do. You can't put PHP code into your content editor, so shortcodes do all the work of a PHP function in an easily writable fashion. A very simple example of a shortcode might be a blog that needs a legal disclaimer at the end of any post written by a lawyer.

There are several ways to do this, but a shortcode is a quick and simple solution. The author of the post could put [disclaimer] in the content editor at the bottom of every post. The shortcode API would interpret this as a call to a PHP function, run that code, and return the preset disclaimer as content. There are hundreds of ways to use shortcodes, and since they even accept parameters, you can do a lot with them.

A Shortcode Example

Let's create a simple shortcode for the legal disclaimer example above. First we'll define the shortcode and the corresponding function to perform in the functions.php file. Then we'll use the shortcode in some content.

Start by opening functions.php. Remember to try and keep your related code consolidated and neat, and comment your code as much as possible so that everyone reading it, including you, will understand the where and why. Insert the following code:

```
add_shortcode( 'disclaimer', 'j2theme_legal_disclaimer' );
```

Here we're calling a WordPress function called add_shortcode(). This function accepts two parameters: the title of the shortcode and the function to call when the shortcode is implemented. For more information on add_shortcode, go to **http://wdgwp.com/add_shortcode**.

Next, create the j2theme_legal_disclaimer function. In this function we want to return some HTML markup with the disclaimer content, so place the following code above the add_shortcode() function:

```
function j2theme_legal_disclaimer(){
  return '<small>Before taking any legal advice you should always consult an
      attorney.</small> ';
}
```

This code is really no different from many of the other PHP functions we've talked about in this book. It performs one task and returns the <small></small> tags for outputting with the rest of the content.

Finally, implement the shortcode. Go to any posts and insert [disclaimer] into the content. Remember the content between the square brackets is the name of the shortcode you defined in the add_shortcode() function. **Figure 17.1** shows the shortcode implemented in a fake post.

FIGURE 17.1 Inserting the [disclaimer] shortcode.

This outputs the following HTML:

```
<p>Welcome to my legal blog. Here we give a ton of legal advice and offer a
    lot of help to our readers. Thanks for visiting and please comment
    and share often.</p>


<small>Before taking any legal advice you should always consult an attorney.
    </small>
```

Since shortcodes return HTML anywhere we place them, we can insert [disclaimer] in the middle of a paragraph. This lets the attorney insert the disclaimer alongside the specific text that's being referred to.

FIGURE 17.2 Inserting the [disclaimer] shortcode mid-paragraph.

Figure 17.2 shows the disclaimer shortcode in the middle of the content that outputs the following HTML:

```
<p>Welcome to my legal blog. Here we give a ton of legal advice and offer a
    lot of help to our readers. <small>Before taking any legal advice you
    should always consult an attorney.</small> Thanks for visiting and
    please comment and share often.</p>
```

You can create many shortcodes to perform multiple tasks. There really are no limits on the number of shortcodes you can write into your theme or plugin.

A Shortcode with Attributes

In this example, we'll add some functionality to the shortcode by giving the user admin the ability to pass parameters to our function. Let's create a shortcode that returns the embed code needed to frame in a Vimeo video.

> ■■■ **NOTE**
>
> oEmbed lets you easily embed videos and other media with associated sites. You can embed Vimeo, YouTube, and other videos simply by placing the video URL in the content editor. You can read more about oEmbed at http://wdgwp.com/oembed. (We're creating the same function with our shortcode, as an example.)

When you copy the following code into your functions.php file, you're declaring a new shortcode called "vimeovid" that calls the custom j2theme_vimeo_vid() function:

```
add_shortcode( 'vimeovid', 'j2theme_vimeo_vid' );
```

When placed above the add_shortcode() function, this function returns the <iframe> markup needed to embed the Vimeo video:

```
function j2theme_vimeo_vid( $atts ){
  return '<iframe src="http://player.vimeo.com/video/{$atts[id]}?title=0&a
      mp;byline=0&amp;portrait=0&amp;color=ff3333" width="{$atts[width]}"
      height="{$atts[height]}" frameborder="0" webkitAllowFullScreen
      mozallowfullscreen allowFullScreen></iframe>';
}
```

This time things may appear a bit different. We're still "returning" some markup, but now we have variables in place of some of the content. Take note that this function now accepts the parameter $atts, which lets you pass variables from the shortcode to the function. These parameters come to the function in the form of an array. Since we're using the PHP return statement we can evaluate the $atts array with curly brackets. This may seem a bit advanced, but let's walk through it.

Now that our functions are in place, we can insert a shortcode into the content. The short-code in **Figure 17.3** looks similar to the previous example, except this time it has specific parameters and values assigned inside it.

FIGURE 17.3 Video shortcode with parameters.

When we pass a parameter of id with the value of "28730350" into our function, the $atts array will hold the key/value pair. We can then return the value of the id by writing {$atts[id]}. The curly braces let us evaluate the array before it's returned.

Inserting [vimeovid id="28730350" width="500" height="375"] into the content editor outputs the following HTML. Notice that the ID, width, and height in the HTML exactly match the parameters passed in the shortcode:

```
<iframe src="http://player.vimeo.com/video/28730350?title=0&amp;byline=0&amp;
        portrait=0&amp;color=ff3333" width="500" height="375" frameborder="0"
        webkitAllowFullScreen mozallowfullscreen allowFullScreen></iframe>
```

When you write your shortcodes, you can replace any parameters you pass with in the square brackets of the $atts array. There are several ways to parse that array—this is just one suggestion.

This code example makes it easy for a user admin to embed a Vimeo video and change the width and height of the <iframe>. You can translate what we did here to any number of examples and build out a great deal of added functionality in your theme.

Enclosed Shortcodes

In the code example above, we created an opening and closing shortcode so we could wrap it around content. In the next chapter, we'll use this technique to show and hide content based on whether or not a user is on a mobile device. For now we'll just wrap some arbitrary content in a <span></span> tag to get used to writing shortcodes like this.

Let's assume the theme does something unique to any <span> tag with a class of "featured." Instead of forcing the user admin to know or write HTML to add this benefit we can instruct him to use our shortcode.

> ■■■ **NOTE**
>
> Shortcodes can be placed in both the visual and the HTML editor. The shortcode is evaluated upon the rendering of content in The Loop, so it doesn't matter how the shortcode is placed. This is because the shortcode isn't really code or markup—it's like more like a WordPress hook that we create.

Insert the following code into the functions.php file, as we've done twice already:

```
function j2theme_span_wrapper( $atts, $content='' ){
  return '<span class="featured">{$content}</span>';
}
add_shortcode( 'spanwrap', 'j2theme_span_wrapper' );
```

Then use the add_shortcode() function to create the shortcode and the function call. In the function j2theme_span_wrapper(), you're now passing a $content as a new parameter and you'll "return" the content wrapped in the <span></span> tags for output.

FIGURE 17.4 Enclosed shortcode.

Figure 17.4 shows the new shortcode wrapped around some content. Notice that the closing shortcode uses a / (forward slash) similar to the URLs of HTML markup. Inserting this code outputs the following HTML, which gives the user admin the desired effect:

```
<p>Here is some <span class="featured">Featured Content</span> that will be
    displayed in some really cool manner.</p>
```

These examples should help you understand building shortcodes into your themes and plugins. Since these were just learning examples you can remove the shortcodes from your functions.php file. We'll create our shortcodes in the next chapter. For more information about the shortcode API, go to http://wdgwp.com/shortcode_api.

Shortcodes are widely used in WordPress. Some great plugins, like Contact Form 7, rely heavily on shortcodes to make it easy to embed forms throughout a site. If you've used WordPress in the past you probably implemented a shortcode, possibly without even knowing it. From now on take special care to note if you're implementing some added functionality by wrapping content in square brackets.

Custom Functions

A semantic and well-thought-out theme will often pull segments of code out of template files and replace them with functions. For example, many of our template files use the same code for our loop. If the loop code is the same then it only makes sense to isolate it to a single location. This way if we have to make a change to it we need only do it once, not multiple times.

Advanced WordPress theming is beyond the scope of this book, so for now we'll use this strategy on a single WordPress call to build a foundation. You can build on this example throughout the theme if you so choose.

We're going to write a custom PHP function to create pagination navigations in our theme. Instead of duplicating this WordPress call in several template files, we'll be able to call a single function we create.

Start by jumping back into the functions.php file. Here, we'll create our function and return our paginated links. The following code is the most advanced we'll write in this book. Go ahead and copy it, then we'll go over it in detail:

```php
function j2theme_paginate() {
  global $paged, $wp_query;
  $abignum = 999999999; //we need an unlikely integer
  $args = array(
    'base'            => str_replace( $abignum, '%#%',
        esc_url( get_pagenum_link( $abignum ) ) ),
    'format'          => '?paged=%#%',
    'current'   => max( 1, get_query_var( 'paged' ) ),
    'total'     => $wp_query->max_num_pages,
    'show_all'        => False,
    'end_size'        => 2,
    'mid_size'        => 2,
    'prev_next' => True,
    'prev_text' => __( '&lt;' ),
    'next_text' => __( '&gt;' ),
    'type'      => 'list'
  );

  echo paginate_links( $args );
}
```

The first line defines the function with the name j2theme_paginate. The second line uses PHP global scope to give us access to $paged and $wp_query values. Sometimes putting code inside a function is like stocking a bunker: The only supplies (variables) you'll have access to are the ones you bring into the bunker (function) with you. Using the global scope property we can gain access to the values that are defined outside the function. For more on PHP and scope, go to http://wdgwp.com/scope.

Next, create a variable called $abignum, which we'll need for the function to perform some calculations. Just create a very large number that will be unlikely to ever be used in a pagination nav. The next line starts an array that we'll fill with parameters to be passed to the paginate_links() function. This function accepts many parameters, some of which may be a bit confusing because we're actually performing functions inside of functions inside of parameter calls. Here's a list of links that provide detailed documentation on everything we just used:

- str_replace()—http://wdgwp.com/str_replace

- esc_url()—http://wdgwp.com/esc_url

- max()—http://wdgwp.com/max

- get_query_var()—http://wdgwp.com/get_query_var

- __() - http://wdgwp.com/_2

- paginate_links() - http://wdgwp.com/paginate_links

The last bit of this function echoes what is returned by the paginate_links() function, which means that anywhere we place the following code, our paginate function will run and return the pagination navigation:

```php
<?php j2theme_paginate(); ?>
```

Make sure you call the j2theme_paginate() function in The Loop. Go ahead and replace the pagination static markup in the theme files with this function. Below is an example of the HTML this function will output. It will vary depending on the number of pages of content the site has to display:

```html
<ul class='page-numbers'>
  <li><span class='page-numbers current'>1</span></li>
  <li><a class='page-numbers' href='http://localhost/j2-theme/page/2/'>2
      </a></li>
  <li><a class='page-numbers' href='http://localhost/j2-theme/page/3/'>3
      </a></li>
  <li><span class="page-numbers dots">&hellip;</span></li>
  <li><a class='page-numbers' href='http://localhost/j2-theme/page/10/'>10
      </a></li>
  <li><a class='page-numbers' href='http://localhost/j2-theme/page/11/'>11
      </a></li>
  <li><a class="next page-numbers" href="http://localhost/j2-theme/
      page/2/">&gt;</a></li>
</ul>
```

The ability to call a complex function like paginate_links() without having to duplicate the parameters saves a lot of time. You can duplicate this strategy in many other areas of the template files. As an exercise, try locating other areas of duplicated code and replacing them with custom functions. These custom functions don't have to be complex. You can write your own to perform multiple complicated tasks or simply return a value.

Shortcode or Custom Function

Whether you're using a shortcode or a custom function, the goal is to reduce the effort in displaying content or performing some functionality. Shortcodes are typically used by user admins, so they can do something that would otherwise be out of the realm of their expertise. And I often write shortcodes for myself so I don't have to recall specific HTML markup if I'm performing a task over and over again.

> ■■■ NOTE
>
> Using shortcodes in widgets is not inherently available. You have to activate this ability by placing the following code into the functions.php file:
>
> ```
> add_filter( 'widget_text', 'do_shortcode' );
> ```
>
> Once you do this you will be able to put shortcodes in widgets for an added benefit to the User Admin.

Shortcodes should be used in content, whereas custom functions are meant to be used in theme files. There are ways to use shortcodes in a theme file. For example, the code below performs our Vimeo shortcode functionality in a template file:

```php
<?php echo do_shortcode( '[vimeovid id="28730350" width="500"
    height="375"]' ); ?>
```

Conditional Statements

There may be times when you need to show something in a template file, but only if you're on the home page. At other times you might want to perform a specific function on a post rather than a page or visa versa. Conditional statements let you test for the existence of elements or the user's current location in the theme, then perform an action based on the outcome.

In PHP, an if statement tests for something to be true and, if it is, proceeds. If it isn't, it does something "else." Read more about if statements at http://wdgwp.com/php-conditionals.

Several WordPress functions exist solely for testing these conditions. For example, if you want to display a link in the footer of your site only when the user is on a post, you could write the following:

```php
<?php
  if( is_single() ) {
    echo '<a href="http://domain.com">My Link</a>';
  }
?>
```

In the above example, if the is_single() function returns true, the <a> tag will be echoed. Otherwise nothing will happen. The is_single() function returns true only if the user is currently viewing a post. There are several other conditional tags available, the most common of which I've listed below. To read more about WordPress conditional tags, go to **http://wdgwp.com/conditional_tags.**

- is_home()—http://wdgwp.com/is_home

- is_front_page()—http://wdgwp.com/is_front_page

- is_single()—http://wdgwp.com/is_single

- is_page()—http://wdgwp.com/is_page

- is_category()—http://wdgwp.com/is_category

- is_404 - http://wdgwp.com/is_404

If you master PHP conditional tests it'll be easy to build out your themes using these functions.

What's Next

We've come a long way and are now implementing some pretty advanced code. Shortcodes and custom functions can take your theme to a whole new level. In the next chapter, we'll make the theme responsive. The HTML and CSS are already done; all we have to do is overcome some WordPress-related hurdles so user admins can maintain the integrity of the responsive layout.

Dear Grasshopper,

When I first used WordPress, I thought of it as a simple tool to start my run-of-the-mill technology blog. But as I learned more about what WordPress had to offer and began to take advantage of its capabilities, my site evolved into a means of personal branding and a place for current and potential clients to connect with me.

I'll admit that I'm not a true developer/designer. My clients tend to be people who are just starting with WordPress. I teach them the ins and outs of updating, managing, and maintaining their sites. It can be a challenge, but thankfully they usually have a personal/business focus before embarking on their journey into WordPress. The outcome is, more often than not, very rewarding. For those clients who just want to start a site with no real focus, I encourage them to do some research as to why they want a site, what message they want to convey, and how they want to deliver this message before starting any website work. The heart of a WordPress site is its content. Without it, there's no foundation for development or design work to begin.

Once consultation is complete, I encourage my clients to be active in the WordPress community, to look for additional resources and ideas and build their networks. When I first started, I stumbled across my local WordPress community on Twitter and social media, and quickly found it to be a great place to learn, make connections, and explore more of WordPress. Eventually, because of my involvement with the community, I became an organizer (Boston WordPress meetup and WordCamp Boston) and am now giving back.

Every so often, you'll have a client like me who just wants to learn more about WordPress. My advice is to encourage and give them more guidance so that they, in turn, can help others.

Kurt Eng
kurteng.com | @kurteng

PART 5

Responsive WordPress Theming

By 2014, more than 50 percent of all Internet traffic will come from mobile devices. Every year, we see an increase in screen resolutions and monitor sizes. More and more devices—phones, tablets, computers, gaming systems, televisions—give users the ability to navigate the web. As web designers, we can no longer afford to constrain our websites to stagnant widths and screen sizes. There are now thousands of variations in resolutions, screen sizes, and device types.

Responsive web design is evolving rapidly. Clients are beginning to expect their sites to be responsive. In this part, we'll go through the steps of coding out responsive elements and functionality. WordPress doesn't always make it easy to maintain a theme's responsive layout, but we can do our best to prepare for it.

Ensuring Responsive Integrity

Because of the way that the HTML, CSS, and JavaScript have been built for our theme, it is already responsive for the most part. However, there are some inherent WordPress functions that we have to account for to ensure that the site is accessible on a wide variety of devices. Likewise, there are some advantages to using WordPress when building responsive websites.

We can plan for some of the disadvantages of WordPress like auto-embedding of pixel-based width and height attributes. We can also take advantage of multiple sidebars, menus, and other dynamic elements to create a more intelligent theme. However, we won't be able to account for everything. At some point, it will be the responsibility of the user admins to ensure the integrity of the theme's responsive functionality, so it's essential that you provide them with guidance.

What you're about to learn

■ Responsive theming concepts

■ Advantages and disadvantages of using WordPress with a responsive site

■ How to test for mobile devices using PHP

■ How to create shortcodes to empower user admins

■ How to use JavaScript to fix some problems related to responsive sites

Planning Responsive WordPress Themes

Responsive web design doesn't mean building a website just for mobile devices, but rather placing a renewed focus on content and its delivery. Content can be an article, a video, or even simple contact information, all of which has no value if a user can't digest it because of the limits of a website's adaptation to a device. No matter how beautiful, fast, or interactive your site is, in the end it's no good if the user can't find a phone number, fill out a form, or locate store hours.

It's important to lay out a plan or structure for user admins to enter content or alter the site without degrading our responsive efforts. To that end, we're going to use a lot of what we've discussed throughout this book, including creating alternative navigation menus, using short-codes to hide content, overwriting static size attributes, and more.

Disadvantages

Since WordPress has to be, in a sense, dummy proof, it automatically writes HTML the way it most makes sense. One way this is a disadvantage to responsive layouts is the generating of static pixel sizes on <img> tags. When a user admin uploads an image and inserts it in a post, WordPress generates the necessary <img> tag. Here's an example of the HTML generated by WordPress when we upload an image to a post (generated classes are excluded to save a bit of space):

```
<img src="http://localhost/j2-theme/wp-content/uploads/2012/05/example.png"
    alt="" title="example" width="584" height="371"  />
```

Regardless of whether or not a user is viewing the site on a mobile device, having a static width of 584 (pixels) won't work well with a responsive layout. If the column is significantly wider than the image, we could have a large amount of white space. Worse, if the column is significantly smaller because the viewing window is decreased, the image can break out of the column and essentially ruin the design of the site.

Advantages

WordPress's dynamic nature makes it easy to create alternative content to serve users based on their device or the size of their screen. We've already created menu locations in Chapter 7, "Menus and Navigation." Now we have the potential to create additional locations so user admins can create alternative menus that may be smaller and leaner for viewing on mobile devices.

We can also create shortcodes to empower user admins to take control of their content while maintaining a responsive layout. A static HTML website might not have these abilities built in and could force user admins to learn HTML or deal with a broken site.

Conditional Tests for Mobile vs. Computer

In this section we'll implement some outside code to help us test for device type. A great PHP class called PHP Mobile Detect (which you can read more about at http://wdgwp.com/php-mobile-detect) is free and available for download on GitHub at http://wdgwp.com/download-php-mobile. The code was originally written by Victor Stanciu and is now maintained and managed by Serban Ghita.

Once downloaded, move the Mobile_Detect.php file into the "bin" folder in our theme. This is the first step to accessing this script. Next, open the functions.php file (by now you should see that nearly all our custom functionality has started in this file) and insert the following code:

```
require_once( get_template_directory() . '/bin/Mobile_Detect.php' );
$detect = new Mobile_Detect();
```

The require_once() PHP function pulls in the code from the requested file. The get_template _directory() function locates the location of the theme files. The $detect object holds a new instance of the Mobile_Detect() class. This lets us call it later throughout the theme.

Remember how we created multiple featured image sizes? Well, let's use that as an example of how to implement this code. Locate the following code in the index.php main content loop:

```
<?php the_post_thumbnail( 'post-thumb' ); ?>
```

This pulls in an image 260px × 175px. Having multiple images at this size render on the home page may not be desirable or necessary to a mobile user. With the PHP Mobile Detect code, we can load a different size of the image or choose to remove it altogether. Being able to prevent an unnecessary PHP and database call is a significant gain to the user in both processing and bandwidth usage.

The following code will show only the thumbnail if the user is not on a mobile device. Notice the "!" that signifies a "not" conditional:

```
<?php
  global $detect; //global scope for use of $detect from functions.php
  if ( ! $detect->isMobile ) ) the_post_thumbnail( 'post-thumb' );
?>
```

In this version of the code we're using the PHP Mobile Detect code to swap out the larger thumbnail for a smaller, optimized version:

```php
<?php
  global $detect; //global scope for use of $detect from functions.php
  if ( $detect->isMobile ) ) the_post_thumbnail( 'sm-post-thumb' );
  else the_post_thumbnail( 'post-thumb' );
?>
```

These are simplified but completely practical examples of how to use the PHP Mobile Detect class to alter your site based on a user's device. There are several additional functions available in the class to detect specific devices like phone versus tablet or test against operating system like iOS versus Android. Take an in-depth look at this class so you can get a better understanding of all the things you can test for.

The following code structure can be used throughout the theme to offer alternative content using the PHP Mobile Detect class:

```php
<?php
  global $detect;
  if ( $detect->isMobile() ) {
?>
    <!-- HTML CONTENT FOR MOBILE -->
<?php
  }
  else {
?>
    <!-- HTML CONTENT FOR NON MOBILE -->
<?php
  }
?>
```

Your theme can provide a great deal of support to the user admin, giving her greater control over the content and when it's displayed. Consider having multiple featured thumbnails in different sizes but identical ratios for easy swapping of images. You can also offer multiple nav locations and swap them based on conditions. The content will not be duplicated on the client side, so you'll be using SEO and semantic best practices.

Shortcodes for Responsive

We can build on the PHP Mobile Detect script to create shortcodes to better manage our content. A wrapping shortcode that goes around anything that's not meant for mobile users will come in handy for the user admin. Maybe the user admin has created a huge info graphic that has no practical way of being optimized for mobile devices. We can create a shortcode that wraps these elements to prevent them from showing on mobile devices. Alternatively, we can create a shortcode that holds content meant only for mobile, such as mobile-optimized versions of content or a link to download a large graphic instead of auto-displaying it:

```
function j2theme_nomobile( $tats, $content="" ) {
  global $detect;
  if( ! $detect->is_Mobile() )return "{$content}";
}
add_shortcode( 'nomobile', 'j2theme_nomobile' );
```

The above code returns only the content for outputting if the user is not on a mobile device. Otherwise it returns nothing, essentially removing the content wrapped in the shortcode tags. **Figure 18.1** shows how this looks in the editor.

FIGURE 18.1 Implementation of the [nomobile] shortcode.

A problem may arise if all the surrounding content is referring to the infographic. Now we've taken away from the experience for the mobile user. Instead, let's provide an alternative for that content and create an [onlymobile] shortcode:

```
function j2theme_onlymobile( $atts, $content="" ) {
  global $detect;
  if( $detect->is_Mobile() )return "{$content}";
}
add_shortcode( 'onlymobile', 'j2theme_onlymobile' );
```

With only a slight change in the code, we've created an easy alternative to the large info-graphic. **Figure 18.2** shows the proper use of the shortcodes.

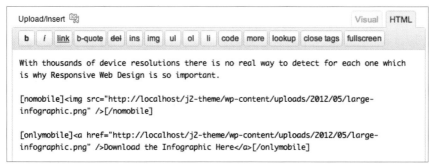

FIGURE 18.2 Implementation of the [onlymobile] shortcode.

Since these two shortcodes are paired together, they will work together to provide an alternative for the user. This doesn't mean they always have to be together. The user admin could use the [nomobile] shortcode on anything she doesn't want displayed on a mobile device. A Google AdWords script might not make sense on a mobile device or have an alternative.

Overwriting WordPress Markup

As we discussed earlier, sometimes WordPress works against your efforts to build a responsive theme. When a user admin uploads media, WordPress appends a pixel-based size attribute. Hard coding the width of an image into a fluid column is not a good idea. The problem is we can't count on the user admin to know how to fix this. Right now there's no perfect solution. We can write some JavaScript to remove the width and height attributes, but this won't always solve the problem. We could replace the pixel dimension with a percentage, but we can't always assume that the user admin wants the image to be one size in relation to its parent.

A more complex solution might be to test the image size against the parent size, and then try to make an assumption about how the user admin was trying to make the image look in relation to the content—but this will never be perfect.

Image Uploader

Figure 18.3 shows an example of the choices that the user admin has when uploading and inserting an image into the content editor. These sizes are based on the width and height dimensions set in the settings or by the developer in the theme. Either way, there are no choices for percentages. Even if we add percentage widths, we'd still have to give the user admin the ability to choose the right image. For example, a user admin might select the small thumbnail 150px × 150px. If the user admin matches that with a 100% wide attribute, then the image will be greatly distorted. This whole process can become very confusing.

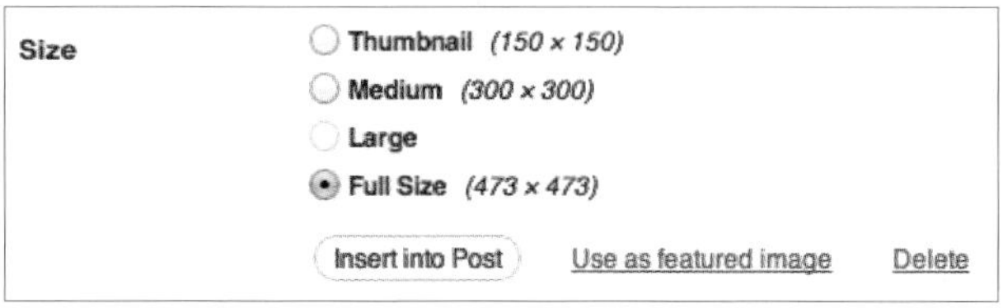

Size	
	○ **Thumbnail** *(150 × 150)*
	○ **Medium** *(300 × 300)*
	○ **Large**
	◉ **Full Size** *(473 × 473)*
	(Insert into Post) Use as featured image Delete

FIGURE 18.3 Image uploader.

It's a good idea to test your own solutions for your sites and themes. As an advanced solution (beyond the scope of this book), you could replace the choices in the image uploader with more flexible, fluid image sizes.

Overwrite with JavaScript

As a last resort, you could use JavaScript to seek out hard-coded pixel dimensions on images and replace them with pixel-based dimensions. In two lines of jQuery we can remove the hard-coded pixel width and height attributes. The following code is a basic example of how to accomplish this:

```
$(function() {
  $(".post img").removeAttr("width").removeAttribute("height");
  $(".post img").width("95%");
});
```

This JavaScript can be placed in any .js file and put into the theme folder. We can call it in the header as we do with other files. The script finds all <img> tags within any element using the "post" class. The attributes are removed and the image is given a width of 95%.

> **BEST PRACTICE**
>
> When using jQuery or other scripts, it's important to enqueue them. This is, in a sense, registering the script so you're not calling it multiple times or overwriting versions. jQuery is good example of a script that should be enqueued, especially since it's used so often in both plugins and themes. For more information on enqueuing, go to http://wdgwp.com/enqueue.

You can adopt and modify this script for your theme. Many areas of the site may require attributes to be repaired with a script like this. Featured images, for example, have hard-coded dimension attributes on the <img> tags. You can call these individually and replace the respective attributes as needed.

What's Next

Unfortunately, there's no be-all and end-all answer to making a WordPress theme responsive, but these techniques will take you nearly all the way. In the next chapter, we'll tidy up our theme, code some additional functionality, and prep everything for launch. We're almost there.

Dear WordPress University Underclassman,

Giving back is good for WordPress and good for you. As you become more involved with WordPress, you'll learn that it's more than just software—it's a community. The biggest mistake you could make is regarding this community as an optional feature. Giving back doesn't just make you feel good—it's a great way to become known as an expert. Releasing a free plugin or theme can take time away from client work, but it can also yield leads for years to come. I had an idea for a plugin one night. It took about four hours to code it and release it. Within weeks, it led directly to a new client. I wouldn't have gotten that client if I hadn't given back.

Have you encountered a difficult problem in WordPress and solved it? Share your solution in a blog post! Someone else is having that same issue, and when he finds your post, he'll think of you the next time he runs into trouble. New clients won't ask to see a sample of your work, and you'll spend less time convincing people that you know what you're talking about. We learn best by doing. Sharing your knowledge and the fruits of your labor is a really powerful way to advertise your skills.

Getting involved with the WordPress community will also give you access to a professional support network. These are people who can give you valuable advice, save you time and effort, and help you find new opportunities. Go to a local WordPress meetup or a WordCamp event. Meet other people who make things with WordPress. Stay in touch with them.

Get involved. Show your work Give back. Share knowledge. Connect. And have fun!

Welcome to the WordPress community.

Mark Jaquith
markjaquith.com | @markjaquith

PART 6
Joining the Community

WordPress stands alone in regards to the size and strength of its community. Other CMSs don't even come close to the number of members, developers, and events around the world. The reason for this is culture. Much like that of a great startup or corporation, the culture is everything.

WordPress is GPL, free to use and open to contributions from everyone. This lays the framework for a great culture and community. Layered on top of that is a large group of Master-level developers are continually giving of their time, knowledge, and expertise in WordPress forums, mailing lists, and events—to benefit individuals and the entire community.

Taking things one step further are WordPress meetups and WordCamps, events where anyone can organize, attend, or speak. WordPress and Automattic empower you to build your own local community, to strengthen the global one.

In this part of the book, you're going to learn how to utilize resources at your disposal to test and launch your site. After that, you'll find out just how easy it is to join the WordPress community. As I tell my students, I only have so much time to teach you WordPress. Instead I'd like to teach you how to learn WordPress then you can keep it going for years to come.

Test and Launch

We're nearing the end of theme development. There are still a few functions to write and some additional functionality to activate, but we're close. Luckily, WordPress has a development checklist to help us make sure we haven't missed any important details.

Once we finish development, we can pack it up and activate it on any WordPress install. Since we've worked hard to keep the content independent of the theme, there won't be much that requires our attention once we upload the theme. However, it will become obvious once the theme is live that it's never really done and that there's always room for improvement.

What you're about to learn

- How to implement the post_class() function

- How to add theme support for a custom header and background

- Techniques for testing your theme

- How to prep your theme for repository submission

Odds and Ends

As we come to the end of our project, there are a few things we need to make sure were done. If you look at the WordPress theme development checklist (**http://wdgwp.com/checklist**), you'll see that nearly everything is complete except for a few minor details.

Let's go through the theme and the checklist and pull out anything we might have left behind. No matter how much experience you have in theme development, it's common to forget a thing or two. That's why this checklist is a good reference. You should also start your own checklist that's customized for your process.

Post Class

Post classes need to go on all HTML elements that house a post. For example, on the home page (index.php) we use the <article> tag in The Loop for all posts. To generate the necessary classes for all our posts, we'll use the post_class() function:

```
<article id="post-<?php the_ID(); ?>" <?php post_class(); ?>>
```

The code above should replace the opening <article> tag in The Loop. Not only are we using the post_class() function, which generates all the necessary classes, we're also creating an ID for the post. The the_ID() function returns the current post's ID. This will give each post a unique ID of "post-#". For more information on post_class() and the_ID(), go to **http://wdgwp.com/post_class** and **http://wdgwp.com/the_id**.

Make sure to go through your template files and replace the containing HTML elements classes and IDs with these calls. If you want your own custom classes, you can always pass them through the post_class() function as we did with the body_class() function at the beginning of this book.

Custom Header and Background

As of WordPress 3.4, it's necessary to add custom header and background functions using the add_theme_support() function. Custom headers and backgrounds give added support to the user admin by making it possible to upload custom images and modify settings to augment the theme design.

Add the following code to the functions.php file:

```
add_theme_support( 'custom-header' );
add_theme_support( 'custom-background' );
```

Once this code is in place you'll notice two new menu items under the Appearance section of the admin. As seen in **Figures 19.1** and **19.2**, the user admin can now upload a custom image for the header. He can also upload a custom background image and add a background color.

FIGURE 19.1 Custom header options.

Custom Background

Background Image

Preview

Upload Image

Choose an image from your computer:

Choose File No file chosen   Upload

or

Choose from image library

Display Options

Background Color   #   Select a Color

Save Changes

FIGURE 19.2 Current background options.

For more information on customizing these settings and displaying the resulting content on your theme, go to http://wdgwp.com/custom_headers and http://wdgwp.com/custom_backgrounds.

Edit Post Button

On the checklist you'll see "Display an Edit link for logged-in users with edit permissions" for pages and single posts. You've probably seen the Edit button before—nearly all themes have it. This button usually appears on posts just below the content area for logged-in users who have the right level of permission. This is basically a quick link for the user admin to navigate to the Edit Post page so he can modify something on the fly.

In true WordPress fashion this is achieved simply by coding a WordPress Template Tag. Insert the code below in The Loop just below the call for content on your single and page template files:

```php
<?php edit_post_link( 'Edit', '<p>', '</p>' ); ?>
```

The edit_post_link() function accepts a few parameters, the first of which is what content will reside between the <a></a> tags. The latter two parameters hold the HTML markup for what goes before and after the link. You can view the edit_post_link() function details at http://wdgwp.com/edit_post_link. The HTML will be output when the user admin views the post:

```html
<p><a class="post-edit-link" href="http://localhost/j2-theme/wp-admin/
        post.php?post=5&amp;action=edit" title="Edit Post">Edit</a></p>
```

Theme Thumbnail

In the beginning of our theme development project, we modified the beginning of the style. css file with the theme details. We changed the name, author, and description of the theme. The last step to finalizing the theme description is to add a thumbnail to the theme file directory.

Create a screenshot of your theme, call it screenshot.png, and add it to the top-level direc-tory of your theme. The recommended dimensions for this graphic are 300 × 225. With the screenshot in place, the theme description is complete. Take a look at **Figure 19.3** to see the theme description in the Appearance → Themes section of the admin.

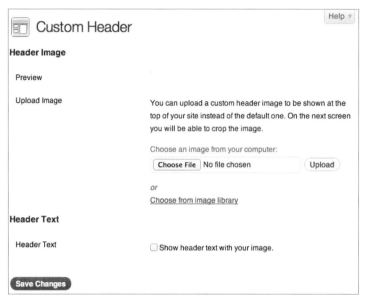

FIGURE 19.3 Current theme description.

Launch!

Are you ready to launch this theme or what? If you're like me, you want to "ship" it and you want to ship it now. My personal feeling is that if you're able to support the theme, then go ahead and get it into your client's hands. There's no better way to find bugs and issues or discover possible feature improvements than to get people using your product.

Testing

Before we launch we need to do some theme development and usability testing. As long as there are no major issues, you should feel comfortable launching the theme.

You've built websites in the past, so you know how to test for cross-browser compatibility problems, look for issues with mobile devices, and do some speed tests. With those out of the way, the next step is to browse the site as a user, search for content, click on categories, and use the pagination—just click on anything you can find.

If you have no issues there, go through the WordPress back end, add content, upload images, and navigate around the admin. Finally, take some time to go through the checklist at http://wdgwp.com/testing.

One thing that every developer should do is the Theme Unit Test. Go to http://wdgwp.com/unit_test and get the data export .xml file. Once you have the file, import it into your testing WordPress environment and follow the instructions on the same page. This .xml file imports fake content so you can do a thorough and complete test of your theme.

Assuming everything goes well, the last thing to do is activate the theme. Well, guess what? You've already done that. We did it way back in the beginning of this book. Since we were diligent about keeping the content independent of the theme, we actually have nothing more to do than put the site live. Just upload the theme and activate it. You'll have to go in and read your widgets and modify your site settings, but that's really it.

Theme Submission and Review

One of the best ways to give back to the WordPress community is to contribute a theme or plugin to the free theme repository. The theme we've built will end up there when we're finished with it. When you build a WordPress theme and submit it to the repository, you're giving it away to be used as anyone sees fit. There are some licensing guidelines that both you and the user admins should abide by. These are discussed in detail at http://wdgwp.com/licensing.

Submitting your theme for review by the WordPress Theme Review Team can be done at http://wdgwp.com/theme_upload. Before you upload, you'll definitely want to go through the review process checklist. Nearly everything in this list was covered in this book, but there are some serious details and specifics that you need to go through step by step. The WordPress Theme Review Team works hard to make sure that the themes accepted to the directory are of the highest quality.

One element of the review process is that every reference to WordPress must be spelled correctly. Here's a quote from the Theme Review Checklist that speaks to the seriousness of the review process:

CORRECT SPELLING OF WORDPRESS

Themes are REQUIRED to spell "WordPress" correctly in all public-facing text: all one word, with both an uppercase W and P.

For the full theme review checklist, check out **http://wdgwp.com/review**. Also check out the Theme Review Team's main website at **http://wdgwp.com/theme_team**. There are some huge advantages to giving away your theme on the repository. If you can submit a theme here, you have refined your WordPress development skills to a superior level. Having themes in the repository is something to put on a resume or in your portfolio—it's essentially a badge of honor. Clients often flock to well-known developers or to individuals who have built themes they already use, so having a theme in the repository will likely bring you business.

What's Next

Our theme is done and it's live, so we should be done, right? Well, yes, we're done with the project, but we'll never be done learning. In the next chapter, we'll look at resources that are available to help you continue your education. We'll also talk about the community and ways to not only join, but also contribute.

Dear Eventual WordPress Core Contributor,

Two of the best pieces of advice I've received over the years have really impacted my career and I like to share these words of wisdom anytime I can.

The first is: "Don't be afraid to fail." It happens to the best of us, and that's OK! As long as you learn from the experience and apply the knowledge you've gained going forward, you really haven't failed. It was merely a setback.

The second is: "Don't be afraid to release/open source a project." I've always shared my code within my circle of developers and designer friends and colleagues. But there was always some excuse or apprehension in releasing my plugins, themes, and other projects as open source to the community. Is the code good enough? Should I add in this feature before I release? (Anyone in my circle will tell you I am notorious for feature bloat.) Maybe performance could be better? Insert any number of excuses here. One of the things that really pulled me into WordPress was the community, both online and at local WordPress meetups, bootcamps, and other events. The community made the transition from the other communities I was a part of (jQuery and Flash) very easy. This was the reason I let go of my grip on my code and have more actively shared my projects with the world. They may be used by the masses; they may be used by only one other person besides me. Either way, it's good for me and good for you.

Let's take it back a step. Maybe you're just jumping into WordPress and you haven't developed the next "Big Thing." That's OK. It could be as simple as sharing a solution to a problem that you finally figured out or posting a useful snippet of code on your blog or wordpress.org. Helping out a fellow WordPresser with simple constructive feedback is really great too.

All that being said, you can always share with me what you think and what you've worked on.

Aaron Ware
linchpinagency.com | @aaronware

WordPress
Community

We're at the end of the road. What do we do now? This chapter is dedicated to answering exactly that. The WordPress community is robust and welcoming—trust me, you'll fit right in. There are so many ways to contribute, resources to help you learn, and events where you can get involved. You'll never be alone.

What you're about to learn

- Details about the WordPress community

- Where to go for help

- How to contribute

- Ways to stay in touch and get involved

WordPress Resources

Since WordPress is open source, it promotes the contribution of code, documentation, tutorials, examples, and more. Designers and developers take pride in their contributions to an array of resources. Below are some of the more popular resources available to you, but there are countless websites out there.

Codex

We've discussed the codex in great detail and linked to countless functions, Template Tags, and best practice docs. The codex is a robust repository of data all about WordPress and how to use it, build on it, and improve it.

One thing you might not know is that you can contribute to that documentation with content, code examples, or links to great tutorials. Not unlike Wikipedia, the WordPress Codex contains information written by hundreds—if not thousands—of different WordPress developers from around the world.

If you're interested in contributing to the codex, go to **http://wdgwp.com/contribute_codex**, which gives you all the details on how to get started.

Forum

Another great resource for getting answers is the WordPress Forum, which we've discussed in earlier chapters. Just remember to post your questions in the right forum categories. There's no better way to get ignored than asking a basic admin question in the advanced development category.

The forum is a great way to stay connected with the community. Nearly everyone who uses WordPress visits the forum at one time or another. It's a great opportunity to get noticed as well. You can contribute to the forum and answer questions, help others, and make a name for yourself. It's not uncommon to get work, notoriety, or build a reputation by answering questions and helping in the forum.

If you're interested in contributing to the forum, go to **http://wdgwp.com/contribute_forum**.

Mailing Lists

I get the most help with my advanced questions by using the WordPress Hackers Mailing List. There are several mailing lists, but the hacker list is my personal favorite. When you subscribe to a mailing list, you'll be emailed every time someone submits a question. Since there's a large following behind every mailing list, you often get detailed and intelligent answers very quickly.

The mailing list acts as a "group notifier," bcc'ing everyone on the list. If you have a solution or some advice, you can reply to the originating party. When someone asks an interesting or outside the box question, it often sparks a thread with some really outstanding discussions.

This is another place to get noticed and build a reputation. To learn more about mailing lists and see the different ones that are available, go to http://wdgwp.com/contribute_mail.

WordPress IRC

The WordPress IRC lets you get involved in live discussions. IRC stands for Internet Relay Chat, which was around way before AIM or Google Talk. You'll need to get an IRC client and subscribe to the #wordpress channel.

This is a great way to hang with other WordPress developers, enthusiasts, and users. For more info on using IRC to connect with the WordPress community, go to http://wdgwp.com/contribute_irc.

Ways to Give Back

There are several ways to give back to the community. We already talked about contributing to the codex, forums, mailing lists, and using IRC to connect. In earlier chapters, we discussed how creating and submitting themes and plugins to the repository benefits the community.

Another way to help is to always remember to return the favor. If I had a penny for every time I helped someone with a WordPress question or problem, I'd be a really wealthy guy. If I had to pay a penny every time I had a question answered, I'd be living on the streets, bankrupt, and using my laptop as shelter. The point is that the community is fruitful and generous. Give as much, if not more, than you receive and we will all continue to make it better, which in turn helps all of us.

WordPress Translation

WordPress software supports many languages, but if you're multilingual you can provide some great support by translating WordPress, that is, actually going through the software and translating the admin and other areas into your language. This is a huge benefit to WordPress users around the world, making it a more intuitive and readily accessible application.

For more information on translating WordPress, go to **http://wdgwp.com/contribute_translations**.

WordPress Testing

WordPress has a core team, but at any time any developer can contribute to the code that makes WordPress run. The other thing we can do is test future releases, report bugs, and even fix the issues you find. The more eyes on WordPress, the better it will be. Instead of complaining about issues (which many people do), you can follow the path of helping and contributing to the solution.

Even if you don't know how to write the advanced code to fix the problem, a properly formatted and thoroughly tested bug can go a long way toward helping the WordPress team. You can read more about how to contribute to WordPress as a developer at **http://wdgwp.com/contribute_dev**.

WordPress Events

I'm a social guy, so I go to as many WordPress events as possible. I even co-organize a local WordPress meetup. Whether it's a local meetup or an international conference, the goals are to educate, engage, and socialize. I love meetups because I get to talk face-to-face with other people who really enjoy WordPress, as do I.

Meetups

WordPress recently took efforts to centralize all the WordPress meetups around the world in a single site. When they partnered with meetup.com, all meetup organizers were given instructions to create an account and put their meetup info on meetup.com. That was sometime in late 2011 or early 2012, so it hasn't been finalized as of the time I'm writing. However, you can easily search the Internet for local meetups, and I encourage you to do this sooner than later.

You might be surprised to find that there's already a WordPress meetup not far from you. Here in New England, I'm within driving distance of four meetup groups that host free, monthly events. For a list of the WordPress meetups on meetup.com, go to **http://wdgwp.com/meet_ups**.

In the unlikely event that you're not near a local meetup, go ahead and start one. What's stopping you?

WordCamps

WordCamps are informal, community-organized WordPress conferences that take place all over the world, often on an annual basis. There are some requirements required to run a WordCamp, one of which is keeping it affordable. Most WordCamps are under $40, which makes it possible for almost anyone to attend.

WordCamps also usually have multiple tracks, giving everyone from novice WordPress users all the way up to advanced developers added value. I love speaking at and attending WordCamps because it's another great opportunity to make connections and meet some really great people.

Sara Cannon (who wrote the Foreword to this book and is a WordPress core contributor) and I met at WordCamp Boston in 2011. Since then we've stayed in touch, shared code and project details, and helped each other as much as possible. This is just one example of a relationship that spawned from a WordPress event.

What's Next?

Well, that's up to you. After 20 chapters, I've taken you as far as I can—for now. You can use what you've learned in this book as the foundation for a career in WordPress development, consulting, site architecture, or even education. As with web design, it's up to you to continue learning and improving your skills. Don't be afraid to get involved in the community and stay in touch. I want to hear from you and learn about your experience with this book. I hope to meet you at a WordPress event someday soon. Until then, have fun WordPress'ing.

Index